87 WAYS to throw A KILLER PARTY

First published in 2011 by Zest Books
35 Stillman Street, Suite 121, San Francisco, CA 94107
www.zestbooks.net
Created and produced by Zest Books, San Francisco, CA

Typeset in Sabon and Bureau Agency
Teen Nonfiction / Entertaining / Games

Library of Congress Control Number: 2010936583

ISBN-13: 978-0-9819733-9-5
ISBN-10: 0-9819733-9-6

CREDITS
EDITORIAL DIRECTOR: Karen Macklin
EDITORS: Karen Macklin and Hadara Graubart
CREATIVE DIRECTOR: Hallie Warshaw
ART DIRECTOR/COVER DESIGN: Tanya Napier
ILLUSTRATOR: Christian Robinson
RESEARCH EDITOR: Nikki Roddy
MANAGING EDITOR: Pam McElroy
PRODUCTION ARTIST: Marissa Feind

TEEN ADVISORS: Emma Herlihy, Celina Reynes, Diana Rae Valenzuela, Irene Xu

Manufactured in China
LEO 10 9 8 7 6 5 4 3 2 1
4500285609

87 WAYS to throw A KILLER PARTY

Melissa Daly

In high school, it's easy to get stuck in a rut with your social life. Mall, movies, same-old, same-old every weekend. But it doesn't have to be that way. All you need is a great outside-the-box night to shake up the status quo and remind you and your friends that these really are the best years of your life.

And you don't need to have a finished basement, rooftop deck, or in-ground pool to throw the year's most memorable party—nor do you need to make it an elaborate affair complete with fancy invitations, tons of people, and agonizing fears about what might happen to your mom's favorite crystal vase. Parties can be anything. They can be small gatherings with close friends, or evenings spent watching movies or making art. They can happen in your backyard, a favorite park, on a road trip, or in a pre-concert stadium parking lot. Of course, ragers can be awesome, too. Whether you're throwing a party that's big or small, the ideas on these pages can help you take it from an average get-together to a night to remember.

Think of this book as your personal party-planning consultant. Inside you'll find everything you need—activities, play-lists, photo booth ideas, recipes, and more—to throw a bash that will go down in history. Want to make your own Mardi Gras? Host an Anti-Valentine's Day soiree? Get all of your friends together for a chocolate tasting party or a winter solstice gathering? This book shows you how to do it. You can also mix and match themes, creating an Old Hollywood Oscars Night or a Cinco De Mayo Tasting Party, or swap occasions, like using a suggested birthday party theme on graduation night. Be creative! And remember:

Almost any day of the year, there's a great excuse for a party.

87 Ways to Party

ONE: Birthday Parties [14]

TWO: Halloween Parties [28]

Westside High
PJ Prom Party

10
J
Q
K
A

THIRTEEN: Sports and Team Parties [136]

FOURTEEN: TV & Movie Parties [146]

1 Star-Sign Soiree

Are you a headstrong Leo? Or a dreamy Pisces? Astrology devotees believe that the position of the sun, moon, and other heavenly bodies at the time of birth can dictate your personality. Whether you think horoscopes are rooted in truth or just plain silliness, it's still fun to honor the anniversary of a friend's arrival into the world with a celebration built around his or her zodiac sign.

Prep

To start, cut out the horoscope pages from a bunch of different magazines and newspapers, frame them or mat them up on poster board, and display them around the room. The rest of what you do will be sign-specific—see the sidebar for the symbol representing each sign, then brainstorm as many foods, drinks, and decorations as you can that relate to that symbol. If the birthday boy or girl is a Gemini, for example, ask people to come dressed as sets of twins. If the sign is Cancer, serve crab dip with chips; Capricorn, goat cheese and crackers. If it's Aquarius, go for a late '60s "Age of Aquarius" theme (a la the classic musical, *Hair*) with tie-dye and peace signs.

Do

Post a chart on the wall listing each sign along with a description of that sign's personality attributes and what other signs make the best romantic fit. (Find this info in an astrology book or website.) Encourage people to search for an astrological match throughout the course of the evening by posing the classic pickup question to everyone they meet: "What's your sign?"

What's Your Sign?

Aquarius (Water-carrier), January 20 – February 18 • Pisces (Fish), February 19 – March 20 • Aries (Ram), March 21 – April 19 • Taurus (Bull), April 20 – May 20 • Gemini (Twins), May 21 – June 21 • Cancer (Crab), June 22 – July 22 • Leo (Lion), July 23 – August 22 • Virgo (Virgin), August 23 – September 22 • Libra (Scales, as to measure weight), September 23 – October 23 • Scorpio (Scorpion), October 24 – November 21 • Sagittarius (Archer), November 22 – December 21 • Capricorn (Goat), December 22 – January 19

2 Super Surprise Party

Surprise parties are great but they do take a bit of extra planning. You're not only coordinating all of the regular things, like food and invitations, but you're also in charge of making sure no one tells the guest of honor what's in store (while simultaneously making sure that he or she is free that evening, and wears something decent to the affair!).

Prep

Snag a cohost, so one of you can bring the guest of honor while the other one manages the party. Then decide where to hold the main event. Your house isn't the only option—consider a barbecue at a lake, an old-school roller rink, or a restaurant. Finally, choose a date. Make sure it's a day that the guest of honor is free (invite him or her out to a decoy event the night of the party, like dinner out or a movie). Remember to coordinate with your friend's family to clear the date and see which family members should be included.

On your invites, make it clear that the party is a secret and tell guests to come up with an alibi ahead of time in case the honoree asks them to tag along on the decoy activity. For bonus points, see if you can get an unexpected out-of-town friend to show up or stock the pond with cute new potential romantic interests for your friend.

Do

If your cohost is bringing the guest of honor at 8, instruct people to arrive only between 7 and 7:45 or after 8:30. Arrange for your cohost to send a text when they're about to arrive, so the party crew can get ready. The rest is easy: Have everyone jump up and yell surprise when your friend walks in!

The Kidnap

For another take on a surprise party, try this: Tell your friend that you're planning something for her birthday, but don't tell her what—only what to wear and when to be free. Then pick her up, blindfold her, and take her to an unexpected activity, like a concert with her favorite band playing or disco bowling with all of her friends. When you arrive, take the blindfold off and have a party guest snap a photo!

3 Old-School Slumber Party

Feeling nostalgic for your tween years, when an exciting Saturday night meant staying up all night with a small group of friends? Or maybe you just want to have a party where you can wear your cozy pajamas. Either way, you can't go wrong celebrating a birthday with an old-school sleepover. But don't just spread out a bunch of sleeping bags and call it a day. Make it a classic, crazy, campy event to remember.

Serve

Depending on when guests arrive, you'll need evening food and breakfast food. For dinner, try English muffin pizzas with assorted toppings. In the morning, make giant pancakes in funny shapes or set up a cereal bar that includes chocolate- and strawberry-flavored milk. Snacks can also be part of the all-night entertainment—who says you can't bake a cake at 3 am when you get the munchies?

Do

Take advantage of the fact that you and your friends are trapped together (in a good way!) all night, and delay the "slumber" part of your party with these activities.

Themed Fun. Pick a theme (say manicures, video game tournament, or quiz night) and ask everyone you invite to bring one item that can be part of that theme (like a nail polish, video game, or quiz books).

Investigation Games. Get some juicy info out of one another with games like I Never (see Ice-Breaker Party, page 86) or reading aloud from a book like *The Book of Questions*.

Film Festival

No slumber party is complete without a stack of DVDs. Here are a few that go with the theme.

Sleepaway Camp (1983) • *Stand by Me* (1986) • *Sleepover* (2004) • A *Nightmare on Elm Street* (2010)

Love Games. Grab a pen and a piece of paper and play a retro love life-predicting game like MASH (Mansion-Apartment-Shack-House) or paper fortune-teller (a pinwheel-shaped origami contraption you operate with your fingers). Find instructions to both online.

Supernatural Games. You've probably tried Light as a Feather, Stiff as a Board, but here's another cool levitation trick called "human diamagnetism gravity antenna levitation": One friend sits in a chair, while four others stand at his or her shoulders and knees. These four place their hands, one on top of the next person's, on the seated person's head. They remove them all at once, place their two forefingers together underneath a knee or armpit of the seated person, and lift. Supposedly, the person goes up as if weightless. Give it a shot!

4 Classic Costume Party

It's great to be among friends with whom you can really be yourself. It's even better to be among friends dressed as someone completely different. That's the allure of the costume party—the chance to escape the everyday you and spend one night in another person's shoes. And what better reason for a costume party than your birthday?

Wear

The possibilities are limited only by your imagination, and can require elaborate outfits or just a small tweak to your usual dress. Here are some possible costume-party ideas.

Letters. Decide on a letter of the alphabet—your initial maybe?—and require that everyone come dressed as something starting with it. Like for M, you could be a mermaid, marine, masochist, MySpace page, mom, measles patient, or Madonna.

Months. Riff off your birthday month to create a theme. For instance, throw a Rock-tober fest, where everyone must come dressed like a famous musician. Or throw a Mo-vember party where everyone (girls included!) has to wear some sort of moustache (provide extras and/or a brown makeup pencil at the door for anyone who wusses out).

Opposites. Get people to dress up as a member of two contradictory groups, like cops and robbers, devils and angels, or nerds and jocks. (Then organize some kind of stand-off between the two groups.)

Geography. Get people to wear the representative dress of their (or their ancestors') native countries. If people have mixed heritages, have them wear a little something from each one.

Personification. These themes ask guests to interpret abstract concepts. One great example is the Subway Party, where everyone comes dressed as a different stop (like in New York City, the 42nd Street stop would be a glam Broadway starlet and the Wall Street stop would be a straight-laced suit-type). Another idea is an Urban Legends party, where you might come as the giant alligator rumored to live in the city sewer system. Half the fun is trying to guess who's what!

From the Big Screen

Need more costume ideas? Check out the party scenes in these films to help brainstorm ideas.

Movie	Type of Party
The Karate Kid, 1984	School Halloween Dance
Romeo + Juliet, 1996	Royal Costume Ball
Ever After, 1998	Royal Masquerade Ball
Never Been Kissed, 1999	Famous Historical Couples Party
Donnie Darko, 2001	Halloween Party
Bridget Jones's Diary, 2001	Tarts and Vicars Party
Mean Girls, 2004	Halloween Party

5 Birth Year Bash

OK, so the styles and trends that were popular when you were born may not yet officially qualify as "retro," but times were still different enough back then for you to have fun recreating that era. At a birth-year party, you'll celebrate all the cool stuff that first came onto the scene the year you were born—including you!

Prep

Gather old celebrity, teen, and sports magazines that came out the year you were born. (This will take some planning, but you can find them pretty cheap online.) Carefully rip off the covers and individual pages from one or two issues and tape them up on the walls; leave a couple intact for the coffee table. Alternately, make photocopies from a library's magazine archives, or search for your birth year online and print out some of the cover stories or fashion spreads you find.

Also, rent DVDs of popular television shows from that year and play them with the sound off on your TV and laptop. For the mid-'90s, think *My So-Called Life*, *Party of Five*, *Beavis and Butt-Head*, and *Beverly Hills 90210* (the original!).

Birth Year Tunes

Put together a playlist of music from your target year—look up the top 40 pop tunes from the week you were born online. For example, for 1993, plan to dance to songs like "Whoomp! (There It Is)" by Tag Team and Snap!'s "Rhythm Is a Dancer." For 1995, play Alanis Morissette's "You Oughta Know," and "Gangsta's Paradise" by Coolio.

Keep it simple by ordering and handing out buttons, T-shirts, or even underwear that say things like "Made in 1997" or "Vintage 1995." (Go to Cafepress.com and search for the year.) Or, make it a costume party and ask guests to dress in clothing of the era. Go with 1990s Seattle grunge rock and have everyone wear ripped jeans and flannel. Or get people to come as a celebrity or topic that made news during your birth year. For example, for 1994, you could dress as figure skater Nancy Kerrigan, who was clubbed in the knee by the bodyguard of her competitor Tonya Harding. For 1996, you could be Dolly the sheep, the world's first successfully cloned mammal.

6 Piece-of-Cake Party

Some sources say that the first birthday cakes were made in ancient Rome and were composed of cereal and wine (the breakfast of champions!) baked on a griddle, and eaten like cookies. Betty Crocker has made a few improvements to this recipe over the years! Today, the mini version—the cupcake—is hotter than ever and perfect for birthday fun.

Prep

On the invite, ask people to scout magazines or cooking shows for cupcake decorating ideas, as each guest will design a cupcake at the party. Then assemble the things you'll need. Here's a basic checklist of essentials.

- Gel food coloring (and small bowls, one for each color)
- Toothpicks (to mix food coloring into icing)
- Plastic piping bags (or cut holes in one corner of plastic zipper bags), at least one per person, but more if you're making more colors than you have guests
- Decorating tips (plain round ones, plus one leaf, one star, and one petal tip)
- "Couplers" and "rings," which hold decorating tips onto each piping bag
- A knife or icing spatula
- A tablecloth you don't mind potentially trashing
- A batch of cupcakes (bake them the day before)
- White buttercream frosting (made from scratch if possible)

Do

Separate the white frosting into bowls for each guest and let everyone mix in a tiny amount of their chosen colors, adding dye till they reach the shade they want. Apply a base layer of frosting to the cupcakes with a knife first, then spoon what's left into piping bags outfitted with the tips of your choice and decorate. (Or you can decorate right on the naked cake if you want. Try to share colors and tips to minimize bag- and tip-washing (for example, fill the bag with the leaf tip on it with green and that's what you'll all use for any stems and vines).

When the masterpieces are finished, upside-down wine glasses of different heights and shapes make great mini cake pedestals!

Decorating Ideas

You could just have a free-for-all, but here are a few ideas to consider.

1. Have each cupcake feature one letter of the birthday person's name.
2. Combine all your cupcakes into one group design like puzzle pieces.
3. However old the birthday person is, make that many cupcakes to decorate. Then, put a candle in each one and line them up to form one "cake" for him or her to blow out.

7 The Big Give

Birthday presents are fun—sometimes. But you can also wind up with a bunch of stuff that you don't like, don't want, and don't know how to get rid of. Save your friend from this fate! With this party, the birthday person gets a new collection of something her or she is really into. Bonus: Shopping is really easy for everyone else!

Prep

There are three basic ways to do a Big Give.

1. Pick a category based on something the birthday person really likes. It could be beauty loot (everyone brings gifts to refill your friend's vanity, like great new brushes, blushes, mascaras, and lipsticks—and then spends the night making her over with them). Or maybe sci-fi flicks to update your friend's prized collection.
2. Partner with your friend's parents. If you find out they're gifting a new iPod to your friend, have everyone make playlists for him or her. If your friend is getting a new Wii, chip in and buy some new games as presents and play them tournament-style at the party.

3. Get gifts that correlate to an upcoming trip. For example, if he or she is heading away to the shore, get everyone to bring presents like flip-flops, sunglasses, a cool towel, or a shell necklace. If your friend's going skiing, the presents could include hats, gloves, scarves, and sweaters. Is your buddy going backpacking around Europe when school lets out? Outfit him or her with a guidebook, sleep sheet, travel towel, and journal.

Go Further With the Theme

Decorate the party space in line with the gifts given. For instance, if the presents are all makeup, set the space up like a salon with fashion mags everywhere. If they're gifts for a tropical vacation, do up the party in a beach theme with lawn chairs and beach balls. For a ski theme, decorate the windows with spray-snow and serve après-ski snacks like cheese fondue and hot cocoa.

8 Heroes and Villains Party

Celts in the first century AD wore some of the first Halloween costumes. They disguised themselves to ward off the ghosts that they believed might return to earth on October 31, the day before the New Year on their calendar. By the year 1000, the top disguises of the day had become angels and demons. Years later, we still love to play with the archetypes of good and evil (aka superheroes and archenemies), so make it a party for good guys and bad guys at your next Halloween shindig.

Wear

Tell guests to come dressed as any hero or villain—real or fictional, modern or old-school, human or other. Be original. For instance, you can come as a villian like swine flu (think: a snout-nose mask and a bathrobe with cold medicine peeking out of the pocket), or team up with others for a group costume like Adam, Eve, and the serpent (get ready to rock some fig leaves).

Serve

Mix up some kryptonite punch as an homage to Superman, arguably the most famous hero of all time. To do this, fill a bowl with lemon-lime soda and jagged chunks of green ice (freeze a container full of Kool-Aid and hack it up in advance). For villainous snacks, bake up cookies in the shape of revolvers (cookie cutters can be found online).

Do

In lieu of a costume contest, have a cage match. Bring up any two heroes or villains at a time and ask the rest of the crowd the age-old question, "Who would win in a fight?" Rocky Balboa or Rambo? Charlie's Angels or The Powerpuff Girls? Iron Man or The Joker? The crowd should vote by applause. Last guest standing can declare the triumph of good over evil—or vice versa!

Set out props like toy weapons, ropes, and a homemade cardboard jail cell, and encourage guests to snap photos of creative stand-offs between the virtuous and the wicked.

The Greats

The American Film Institute has named the top 100 movie heroes and villains of all time. Get costume inspiration from these flicks, or play them on your TV or laptop in the background at the party:

Top 3 Heroes

1. Atticus Finch, *To Kill a Mockingbird* (1962) • **2.** Indiana Jones, *Raiders of the Lost Ark* (1981) • **3.** James Bond, *Dr. No* (1962)

Top 3 Villains

1. Dr. Hannibal Lecter, *The Silence of the Lambs* (1991) • **2.** Norman Bates, *Psycho* (1960) • **3.** Darth Vader, *The Empire Strikes Back* (1980)

9 Haunted Hotel Party

From the Bates Motel in *Psycho* to the Overlook hotel in *The Shining*, scary lodging places that get taken over by ghosts, wackos, or both are a favorite in Hollywood. Riff off this idea for your next Halloween party by converting your space into a creepy inn where guests check in … but they might not check out. Muahh ha haa.

Prep

With a few touches, you can make your home look like a hotel. Turn the bathroom door into an elevator by making a floor dial and up/down buttons to stick above and to the side of it. Scatter homemade "room service" menus around the room listing the items available at the buffet table. Then cover everything with the usual Halloween accoutrements, like cobwebs and fake blood. If you're a devotee of one of the classic films mentioned above, here are a couple of ideas for thematic additions.

The Shining. Serve cherry-colored punch labeled "REDRUM" ("murder" spelled backward). In place of a tablecloth, cover the food table with sheets of paper that have "All work and no play makes Jack a dull boy" typed over and over again. Mark one of the doors inside the house with a sign reading "Room 237." Enlist a friend and dress as one of the creepy Grady twins by wearing matching blue short-sleeved dresses (with or without fake blood spatters) and knee socks.

Psycho. Buy a clear plastic shower curtain, spatter it with red paint, and hang it on a curtain rod in the living room; take photos of guests peeking out from behind it doing their best horror-struck-scream faces. Set a plastic skeleton in an old dress and brown wig in a rocking chair in front of a window a la Norman Bates' dead mom; aim a lamp toward it so arriving guests see the silhouette from the outside. Then, dress like Bates in an ill-fitting thrift-store frock over regular men's clothing, and carry a large, fake kitchen knife.

In-Room Entertainment

Watch these flicks for inspiration, or play them on your TV in the background at the party.

Psycho (1960) • *The Shining* (1980) • *Hotel* (2001) • *Identity* (2003) • *Hostel* (2005) • *1408* (2007) • *Vacancy* (2007)

Do

As people arrive, have them "check in" to the hotel. Post one of your friends at a table near the entrance; he or she will tell guests to sign their names in a guest book and give them some kind of key or card with a room number written on it. (Use the room numbers as raffle numbers for a DVD of your creepy hotel flick of choice!)

10 Murder Mystery Party

Halloween's all about the macabre, so instead of just dressing up like the dead and those who slayed them, act the part. Throw a murder mystery party where a homicide is staged and guests are tasked with figuring out who's the real killer.

Prep

There are two ways to go about it.

Big Mystery (8 or more guests). Come up with a storyline for the evening that involves a cast of characters, including a murderer and a victim. Then, give guests cheat sheets in advance telling them who they are, what kind of costume they should wear, and a few things they should reveal when mingling with other guests. Halfway through the night, turn out the lights and—gasp!—one of your friends (as directed by his or her cheat sheet), falls down dead. By the end of the night, if you've constructed the story well and everyone has played their part, all the necessary clues are out there for someone to put together and guess the murderer. (If you're lacking the motivation to write the story yourself, buy a kit online or from a party store with a professionally written storyline—but it's more fun to make up your own!)

Clue (3 to 6 guests). This simpler setup plays off the board game *Clue*. (If you've never played *Clue*, check out the full rules online or in someone's game.) Have everyone come dressed as one of the characters, and put up signs labeling the rooms of your house as the rooms in the game. Put a suspect, weapon, and room card into an envelope. Distribute the rest of the cards among the guests, then play just like the regular game, using your house as the game board. On each person's turn, instead of rolling a die to move a certain number of spaces on the board, the player will simply choose which room to be in for that turn (i.e., stay put or go to an adjacent room).

The Plot Thickens ...

Here are a few of the best-ever whodunit movies to inspire your script.

Murder on the Orient Express (1974) • *Clue* (1985) • *Seven* (1995) • *Gosford Park* (2001)

PHOTO STATION

While the game may only have one criminal, everyone should get a mug shot! Line a piece of white poster paper horizontally with an inch between lines, and label every third one with a height marker—5'6", 5'9", 6', etc. Hang it on the wall so that the heights are true to life; this will create the backdrop for a traditional mug shot. Then create an identity placard for people to hold up when they get their photo taken. It should read "Sheriff's Office" or "police department," the date of your party, and a five- or six-digit inmate number.

11 Pumpkin-Carving Party

The idea of turning pumpkins into oversize candleholders comes from an Irish legend. It's about a mischievous man named Jack who liked to play tricks on the devil; after he died, his spirit was barred entrance to both heaven and hell, so he's been wandering the planet ever since, carrying a lantern made out of a hollowed-out turnip with a lump of burning coal inside. When the Irish came to America, turnips were replaced with the local produce—pumpkins. These turned out to be even better for carving, as well as a great theme for a pre-Halloween party.

Prep

Ask everyone to bring a pumpkin over or go pumpkin picking together and bring the goods back to your house. Buy votive candles or LED tea lights to put inside each one. Get one pumpkin-carving kit and have everyone share the specialized tools and design ideas. Then set out a bunch of additional small serrated knives, big spoons (flat or round ice cream scoops also work well), and pencils. Lay out newspapers on the floor to protect it from pumpkin guts.

Do

To carve your pumpkin, start by cutting a circle around the stem to create a lift-off lid—angle the knife toward the stem so the lid doesn't fall right through to the inside—then scoop out all of the seeds. Next, sketch your design on the outside with a pencil before cutting. Remember that any solid sections need to be connected by at least a sliver of flesh to the rest of the pumpkin, other-

Halloween Playlist

"Ghostbusters" (Ray Parker, Jr.) • "I Want Candy" (Bow Wow Wow) • "It's Tricky" (Run DMC) • "Thriller" (Michael Jackson) • "Werewolves of London" (Warren Zevon) • "(Don't Fear) The Reaper" (Blue Oyster Cult) • "Devil Inside" (INXS) • "Little Ghost" (The White Stripes)

wise they'll fall right out (gravity and all). When your masterpieces are finished, light them and line them up, and take plenty of pictures. Consider giving out prizes for funniest, scariest, and best-in-show.

Serve

Blend canned pumpkin puree with milk, vanilla yogurt, vanilla extract, and pumpkin pie spice to make pumpkin smoothies. For another snack, coat the seeds from your jack-o-lanterns (separated and rinsed) in vegetable oil or melted butter and spices (either savory, like cumin, or sweet, like cinnamon and nutmeg), and spread them in a single layer on a cookie sheet. Bake at 300 degrees for about an hour, stirring and turning them periodically, until golden brown.

12 Blood Bash

What is it that's so hot about being bitten by a cold, murderous, half-dead corpse? Who knows, but people have been fascinated by vampires for centuries. There are legends of blood-suckers dating back all the way to the first millennium AD in Greece and China. Nowadays, of course, vampires are a whole lot cuter than in past generations, and it may be hard to resist eternal damnation when the opportunity arises for a neck-bite from a mysterious (albeit toothy) beauty at this vampire-themed Halloween party.

Prep

Your costume will depend on which vampire flick is your inspiration: castle stone and coffins a la *Dracula* or something more like the sparkly glitter feel of *Twilight*. Either way, you'll need a lot of red and black. Get a big bolt of black tulle from the fabric store and drape it over your curtains. Cover other sections of the walls with white sheets splattered with red paint. Draw pairs of red eyes to stick on windows (or use store-bought stickers) so vamps appear to be peaking in from outside.

Serve

A big bowl of any red-colored punch will be your centerpiece. Rig up a fake blood bag from the Halloween store (or a plastic zipper bag and some clear tubing from the hardware store) to look like it's feeding into the bowl. Print out pages with the words "O negative" or "AB positive" from your computer, cut them into rectangular labels, and tape them around glasses. Or go fancier by dipping the rims of your glasses in a blood-red syrup, letting it drip down the side to harden. To do this, combine one part corn syrup with one part water and two parts sugar, and heat without stirring on the stove until the mixture reaches 300 degrees. Drop in some red food-dye. Then turn off the heat, and while the mixture is still hot, dip. Watch your fingers!

Onscreen Vamps

Watch these flicks for inspiration, or play them with the sound off at the party.

Dracula (1931, 1992) • *The Lost Boys* (1987) • *Interview with the Vampire* (1994) • *Buffy the Vampire Slayer* (1997) • *Blade* (1998) • *Van Helsing* (2004) • *Twilight* (2008) • *Let the Right One In* (2008)

Do

As guests arrive, give each one a candy necklace to wear. Tell them that at some cue throughout the night (a whistle, a sound bite from your favorite vampire movie, or your DJ yelling "vampire!"), everyone has to turn to the person next to them at that moment and bite a piece of candy off his or her neck.

13 Chrismukkah Party

There was a time when it was rare for people to mix holidays from two traditions, but these days—because of interfaith families, friendships, and communities—more and more people are combining the winter holidays of Christmas and Hanukkah into one big celebration. (Case in point: The kids on *The O.C.* celebrated Chrismukkah every season.) If you've got friends with both religious beliefs (as well as ones who mostly just believe in presents and cookies), throw a party they can all get into.

Prep

First, pick a date. Christmas is always December 25, but the dates for Hanukkah vary slightly depending on the lunar calendar, and can sometimes fall before or after Christmas. So the date for the party might not be exactly on either holiday. To decorate, make the most of the symbols that the two festivals have in common, like candles, presents, and stars. Then bring in some more fun hybrid stuff. Chrismukkah is becoming a holiday in its own right, so there's lots of cute loot out there combining Jewish, Christian, and secular themes, like tree-shaped dreidels, menorahs with candy cane-colored candles, and CDs of Christmas carols performed by a klezmer band. You can also go DIY with an evergreen wreath adorned with both mini tree ornaments and dreidels; use green floral wire from the craft store to attach each piece.

Do

Play cross-tradition games. One fun one is mistletoe Dreidel. Beneath a big sprig of mistletoe, take turns spinning a dreidel. The spinner has to kiss whomever the pointy end faces when it stops—that is, depending on the Hebrew symbol it lands on. *Nun*: Spin again. *Heh*: Steal a quick peck. *Gimel*: Lean in for a real lip-lock. *Shin*: Pass your smooch to someone else (here's your chance to play matchmaker!).

Including Kwanzaa

Kwanzaa, an African heritage holiday created in the US in 1966, is also celebrated during this time of year (from December 26 to January 1). Kwanzaa is often not observed at pan-holiday parties because the founder, Dr. Maulana Karenga, wanted to keep its integrity as a standalone celebration. But people do still include it sometimes. Gifts are generally only given to children and include corn, a unity cup, candles, and books.

Serve

Fry up *latkes* (potato pancakes, the traditional food of Hanukkah) made with the addition of red pepper and zucchini to match the Christmas color scheme. Follow them up with Christmas cookies decorated with blue and white sugars, the colors of Hanukkah.

14 Naughty or Nice Party

Remember that Christmas carol about an omniscient Santa Claus who somehow knows who's been naughty and who's nice? When you were younger, it may have helped your parents get you to eat your peas or stop fighting with your sister. But now that you're older, being a little bit naughty every now and then can be fun. In fact, as a Christmas party theme, it can be quite nice!

Prep

Arrange two separate areas in your house—the Naughty Room, done up in devilish red tones, and the Nice Room, in angelic white. Here are more ideas to differentiate the spaces.

Naughty Room. Fill the space with red poinsettias and mistletoe—lots of it! Hang red, silk, thigh-high stockings from the mantle or banister, replace regular lighting with red light bulbs, and use a laptop or TV to play *Bad Santa*, the ultimate naughty Christmas flick, on mute. For music, check out the Lump of Coal playlist.

Lump of Coal Playlist

"Santa Baby" (Madonna) • "Fairytale of New York" (Amy Macdonald) • "Oi to the World" (No Doubt) • "I Won't Be Home for Christmas" (Blink-182) • "Christmas in Hollis" (Run-DMC) • "Don't Shoot Me Santa" (The Killers) • "Father Christmas" (The Kinks) • "Christmas Wrapping" (The Waitresses) • "Christmas Tree" (Lady Gaga with Space Cowboy) • "The 12 Days of Christmas" (Straight No Chaser)

Nice Room. Deck the halls with angel ornaments and white twinkly lights, hang squeaky-clean white knee socks in place of stockings, play traditional Christmas carols, and switch on *It's a Wonderful Life* in the background.

Serve

In the Naughty Room, stick to red and/or spicy foods like red-corn chips, salsa, and cinnamon spice gumdrops. For the Nice Room, put out sweet, white foods like white-chocolate-covered pretzels and yogurt-based fruit dip.

PHOTO STATION

Position one of your more charismatic friends in full Claus gear in an armchair near the entrance; don't tell anyone in advance who it is—it'll be funnier that way. As people arrive, have them pose for a photo on Santa's lap. After the picture, he'll use his all-knowing powers to determine whether each guest on his lap is naughty or nice. At that point, the guest's name is added to the appropriate list—drawn up on a very official-looking scroll you've made out of poster paper—and he or she is sent to the corresponding room of the party. How do people get into the other room? They have to do something nice … or naughty!

15 Winter Solstice Party

In the Northern Hemisphere, we celebrate the winter solstice every year around December 21. It's the shortest day (and longest night!) on the calendar—and the first day of winter. So, why celebrate? Because, after this, each day gets a little more daylight, eventually leading up to summer! People have partied on this date throughout history, sometimes even staying up until dawn. Now you can keep the tradition alive.

Prep

The solstice is all about the contrast between light and dark, so lighting is a key décor element. You'll get the best ambiance by filling your space with candles. To be safe, make sure they're in candleholders or glass hurricanes, and place them on high shelves where they're less likely to get knocked over. (Have a fire extinguisher on hand just in case.) Or simply use electric candles and strings of white twinkly lights instead.

Do

Start the party with your house pitch black, and lead guests into the party area with a single candle. Once everyone's there, say something to invite the daylight in, and then pass around matches and let everyone participate in lighting the candles. (Or just switch on all the little electric lights at once.) After the ceremony, add additional light to the room if needed.

Also, try these fun solstice activities.

Log Burning. The Norse people of Scandinavia marked the solstice by burning a large log (called a Yule log) and feasting until it went out. If you have a fireplace, designate a Yule log, and have guests toss twigs on it to cast away the cares of the past year and start fresh.

Rich Serve Poor. Ancient Romans celebrated the solstice with a trading-places tradition called Saturnalia: Slaves acted as masters and the rich served them. Ask guests to bring nonperishables for a food drive, and/or have upperclassmen serve cocoa to their younger "masters."

Light It Up Playlist

"Dark and Lonely Night" (Teenage Fanclub) • "Dancing in the Dark" (Bruce Springsteen) • "Prince of Darkness" (Indigo Girls) • "Aquarius/ Let the Sunshine In" (The Fifth Dimension) • "Here Comes the Sun" (The Beatles) • "Walking on Sunshine" (Katrina & The Waves) • "Soak Up the Sun" (Sheryl Crow)

Lucia Procession. On the Swedish solstice-centered holiday of Lucia, a girl is chosen to play the highly coveted role of Saint Lucia, who wears a white dress and a crown of lights on her head and leads a procession bringing coffee, gingersnaps, and saffron buns to the crowd. Create a crown of battery-powered lights, and have a female guest (or someone's little sister) do the honors.

16 Winter Wonderland Party

Maybe you couldn't squeeze your party into the hectic December calendar, or maybe you just want to celebrate the season without a religious excuse. Either way, why not throw a party in January when people are experiencing postholiday boredom—and winter decorations are on sale!

Prep

Create a winter scene indoors. Grab a can of spray snow to frost the corners of the windows, a bag of faux flakes for dusting the floors and surfaces, and as many clear or silvery glitter snowflake ornaments as you can to hang by white ribbons from the ceiling. Cover the couch and chairs with white sheets, and twist white tulle from the fabric store around strands of white lights to make twinkly snow garlands. Replace the bulbs in your lamps with blue ones to cast a twilight glow. Have ice skates, snowshoes, skis, or poles? Display them around the room. Then, light a fire in the fireplace if you have one, or pop in a flickering fireplace DVD.

Wintry Mix

"Ice Ice Baby" (Vanilla Ice) • "In the Cold, Cold Night" (The White Stripes) • "Hazy Shade of Winter" (The Bangles) • "California Dreamin'" (The Mamas & The Papas) • "Winter" (Tori Amos) • "She's So Cold" (The Rolling Stones) • "A Long December" (Counting Crows) • "Cold As Ice" (Foreigner) • "The Thin Ice" (Pink Floyd)

PHOTO STATION

Create a snowdrift scene by pouring white Styrofoam packing peanuts into a blow-up kiddie pool or old, giant cardboard furniture carton that can be spray-painted white. Stick a pair of skis and/or a funny pom-pom snow hat inside. Guests can climb inside and get their pictures taken as a party souvenir (affix a camera on a stool in front of the pit, and set it on automatic).

Serve

Serve food that's white, warming, or both. Think: meringue cookies, powdered sugar donut holes, rock candy swizzle sticks, and white chocolate fondue with pretzel rods for dipping. Create a cocoa bar with a pot of white hot chocolate plus fixings like marshmallows, whip cream, cinnamon, peppermint sticks, and chocolate shavings.

Do

Have everyone rewrap and bring an unwanted gift they got at the holidays for a "Yankee swap." Draw numbers to determine an order; the person who gets number one starts by picking and opening a gift. Each subsequent person can either choose a wrapped gift or "steal" any gift that's been opened so far.

17 Global Warming Party

Everyone's heard about climate change at this point. You know by now that carbon dioxide levels are rising in the atmosphere, causing temperatures on Earth to get hotter. So, a high of 80 degrees in the middle of January? Probably not a good sign—unless it's the night of your global warming-themed party. In that case, kick off your boots and pour yourself a frozen drink. (And raise consciousness about climate change, while you're at it!)

Prep

Pump up the heat in your house to the mid-80s and get your fireplace going if you have one (this will help warm the house and also represent the increased occurrence of of heat waves and wildfires on the planet that many believe are a result of climate change). Play Al Gore's *An Inconvenient Truth* in the background for ambient natural disaster scenery. Fill up the tub in the nearest bathroom, tape up some faux palm trees on each side and throw in a stuffed polar bear riding on a floaty. Then, leave a trail of "carbon footprints," cut from black construction paper, to the hidden oasis.

Serve

Create a punch bowl made to look like the melting Arctic. The night before, put a big bowl of water in the freezer. When it's frozen, run it under hot water to release the ice, then break it into two or three jagged chunks with an ice pick. Use a dab of white icing to stick a toothpick flag on one chunk that says "North Pole," then float them all in a bowl of blue raspberry drink or lemon lime soda with blue food coloring.

Wear

Tell everyone to come wearing beach clothes—bathing suits, shorts, flip flops, and sundresses. When they arrive, they'll have no problem stripping off their coats and scarves in the tropical heat.

Do

Climate change is causing crazy weather patterns, so simulate a storm of biblical proportions about every 20 minutes by flickering the lights on and off and playing a clip of thunder and rain from a nature sounds album. Place little umbrellas in drink glasses as garnishes (they'll carry double meaning!).

Contribute to the Cause!

Use the party as an opportunity to create awareness about climate change. Collect a donation at the door, which you'll give to a nonprofit organization like the Sierra Club to help fund environment rescue projects, or a company like Carbonfund.org to offset the damage of using extra electricity to heat the room and then some. And print out climate change facts to display next to each item of your décor or around the party in general.

18 Mardi Gras Party

Mardi Gras (French for "Fat Tuesday"), like the Brazilian Carnaval (see page 176), happens in New Orleans, Louisiana, right before the Christian holiday of Lent. The point of Mardi Gras is to have a celebration of fun and debauchery before getting all serious and ready for prayer. During the week before Fat Tuesday, there are themed parades along famous streets like St. Charles Avenue and Canal Street, in which people wear outrageous costumes, ride floats, and throw coveted beads into the crowds. Parties galore also happen along New Orleans' famous Bourbon Street in the French Quarter. If you can't make it down to experience the insanity in person, create some of your own!

Prep

Stock up on Mardi Gras beads. Make sure to get a few cool, funky ones to wear in addition to the cheaper, plainer "throw" beads. Then decorate your place in the official Mardi Gras colors: purple (for justice), green (for faith), and gold (for power). Using green and white poster board, make a faux Bourbon Street sign.

Serve

The traditional Mardi Gras delicacy is a "king cake": a circular, coffee cake-like pastry with a little plastic baby doll inside (lots of recipes online). After baking your cake, cut a small hole in it and tuck the plastic baby inside. Then frost the cake and sprinkle purple, green, and gold sugar on top. Whoever gets the slice with the baby can be considered the king or queen of the night!

Wear

Any festive attire works, though it's fun to get creative. People on Bourbon Street are especially partial to feather boas, glittery masks, and of course, beads—that is, when they're not dressed in costumes resembling court jesters and showgirls. Wearing the three Mardi Gras colors is also high fashion on Fat Tuesday.

Do

The main goal during Mardi Gras is accumulating beads—the fancier, bigger, and more unique, the better. Float-riders throw them to onlookers, who then trade them among one another for various things in return. Trade beads at your party for hugs, kisses, candy, dares, or anything you can think of!

Masquerade Ball

Elaborate masks abound at Mardi Gras, adding even more sparkle and mystery to the affair. Consider setting up a mask-making table at your party for guests to create their own works of identity-disguising art. Provide plain, white eye-masks from the craft store, along with glue, feathers, glitter, sequins, and any other accoutrements you can find.

19 Black and White Ball

Author and noted social climber Truman Capote threw the infamous Black and White Ball at the ultralux Plaza Hotel in New York City in 1966. The event was so legendary it was called the "party of the century" for decades. At the original and the imitations that have followed, the rule is always the same: All guests must wear only black and white. Take a cue from Capote and make your next New Year's Eve fete a sophisticated, swanky affair that everyone who's anyone is dying to attend.

Wear

It's right in the name! Though Black and White Balls are often considered formal—guys wear tuxes or suits and girls wear cocktail dresses or gowns—you could have people come in any garb. Just the fact that everyone is in black and white will create a visually stunning scene.

Want to keep it formal-ish? Pick one of these dress codes for the invite.

White tie (or ultraformal). Guys wear tuxedos with white ties, shirts, and vests; girls wear long evening gowns.

Black tie (or formal). Guys wear tuxes; girls should wear formal dresses, long or short. If an invite says black tie optional, it means you can also wear cocktail attire.

Cocktail attire (or semiformal). Guys wear suits and girls wear cocktail dresses.

Dress to impress. Just look nice. Guys most often wear jeans or pants and a collar shirt, and girls might wear a skirt or jeans and heels.

Valet Parking

Capote would certainly have spared his fabulous guests from having to park their own cars, and you can do the same (if you have guests who drive). Put a "Valet Parking" sign in front of your house, and station a "valet," dressed in a white shirt and a vest, outside to park your friends' cars for them.

Serve

For food, whip up some mini quiches, spanakopita, and other bite-size morsels, or buy them frozen at the supermarket. (Another option: Make your food adhere to the dress code as well and serve only black-and-white eats like Oreos and chocolate cake with vanilla frosting; see the Old Hollywood Party on page 118 for more ideas.) For a high-end touch, recruit someone to play server for the evening. Have him or her dress up in black pants/skirt and a white button-down shirt, drape a dishcloth over one arm, and carry trays with your goodies, along with sparkling cider poured in plastic champagne flutes.

20 Rock-Around-the-Clock Party

Believe it or not, even your great-grandmother got down—just to different tunes and with different moves. From big bands to Elvis, punk to techno, celebrate great dance music of the past and present by playing songs from a different era every half hour throughout New Year's Eve.

Prep

To create your musical backdrop, make eight playlists for your party. The first seven should each be 30 minutes long and made up of songs from each decade from the 1940s through the 2000s. The last mix can be as long as you want, and include all your favorite songs from the current decade.

Make a banner for the party room that says "Happy New Year 2013!" (or whatever year it is). Then make up seven extra sheets of paper in the same color as the banner, just big enough to cover the first three digits of the year. On them, write 200, 199, 198, 197, 196, 195, and 194. Tape them on top of the "201" on the banner, one over the other in the order above, so that when you're done, the banner reads "Happy New Year 1943!" As each decade of music ends, you'll strip off a number (see Do). By midnight, you'll have stripped off all the sheets so the current new year shows again.

Wear

Tell everyone to come dressed in the style of a chosen decade, i.e., poodle skirts for '50s rock, leisure suits for '70s disco, leg warmers for '80s pop, and so on.

Do

After each era, have a mini countdown to the "new year." When you hit number one, rip off a layer of your banner, and press Play on the next playlist. For even more fun, learn a dance step from each decade to teach your boogying buddies.

As Time Goes By

Here are some great dance songs representative of each decade to get you started.

8:30 pm: 1940s "Boogie Woogie Bugle Boy" (The Andrews Sisters), "In the Mood" (Glenn Miller)

9 pm: 1950s "Rock Around the Clock" (Bill Haley and His Comets), "At the Hop" (Danny & the Juniors)

9:30 pm: 1960s "Twist and Shout" (The Beatles), "Do You Love Me" (The Contours)

10 pm: 1970s "Get Down Tonight" (KC & The Sunshine Band), "I Wanna Be Sedated" (Ramones)

10:30 pm: 1980s "Take on Me" (a-ha), "Walk Like an Egyptian" (The Bangles)

11 pm: 1990s "Smells Like Teen Spirit" (Nirvana), "1999" (Prince)

11:30 pm: 2000s "Bye Bye Bye" (*N Sync), "I Gotta Feeling" (The Black Eyed Peas)

12 midnight: 2010s Choose your own favorites!

21 Time Travel Party

New Year's Eve is about celebrating the passage of time, so turn it into a truly epochal affair. Host a time travel-themed party, where guests come dressed as if it's 100 years ago *or* 100 years in the future.

Prep

Search online for images of newspapers featuring major events from a century ago, like World War I and the Titanic disaster. Print them out (blow them up on a photocopier if necessary) and display them on one side of the party room, along with vintage newspaper advertisements from back then (find these at online poster shops). For the other side of the room, create your own newspaper-like images with headlines for events that might happen in the 2110s: "December 7, 2114: Mars Invades Venus!"

What to Wear

Guests can dress in general period costumes or be more specific, like a women's suffragette, a Spanish Flu-era nurse, or Charlie Chaplin. Someone could wear a vintage-looking suit or a dress with a life jacket and be a passenger of the Titanic, which sank in 1912. Or two buddies could wear old-school army uniforms and go as British and German WWI soldiers during the Christmas Truce of 1914, when the enemies took a break from shooting at one another to sing carols and play soccer.

As for the future, it's anyone's guess! Typical costumes involve metallics, *Star Trek*-style bodysuits, or extraterrestrial makeup. But you could go with a "statement" costume instead, like something involving a wetsuit to imply a tomorrow where climate change (see Global Warming Party, page 46) has flooded the Earth, or a man with a pregnant belly to show how modern medicine might make it possible for a man to carry a child.

PHOTO STATION

Place a makeshift time machine in between the two sides of the room. Create it by covering cardboard with tin foil, or just rearranging tall furniture, such as bookcases, to form a secluded nook. Then, hang a foil doorway curtain (sold at party stores) on either side. Place two chairs inside and a light of some kind, and decorate the inside to look like the dashboard of the *Back to the Future* DeLorean or the time travel device of your dreams. Duct-tape your camera (set on auto-timer) to the cardboard or sit it on a shelf facing the chairs. Guests come in one side, take a few pictures, then exit on the other side into a different era!

22 Candy-for-Strangers Party

If you've been hanging around with the same classmates your entire life, go to an all-girls or all-boys school, or have simply dated everyone you know that you would ever want to date, it might be time for some new blood. Valentine's Day is the perfect time to widen your (and your friends') social circle. Sure, Mom said never to accept candy from strangers, but what if you put some out for them? Throw a party where everyone has to bring someone they know, but who is new to other people at the party. Instantly, the dating pool has doubled!

Prep

On your invitations, make it known that every guest must bring along someone from another school. It could be a cousin from upstate, a bunk-mate from summer camp, or a friend they volunteered with all last year—it just has to be someone in the same age range who doesn't know most of the people at the party. (No *actual* strangers, though! You want everyone at your party to be cool, nice, and vouched for by at least one person.) Remember, the idea is to give everyone the chance to meet new romantic potentials; current couples are welcome, of course, but each member of the pair should bring a single friend.

Serve

Ask each of your guests to bring a bag of Valentine's Day candy to pour into a communal bowl on the buffet. In exchange, serve them fancy candy-garnished mocktails like cranberry ginger ale in a wine glass with a red gumdrop sitting on the rim, pink lemonade on the rocks with two red licorice whips as straws, or chocolate milk in a martini glass garnished with a toothpick-speared chocolate truffle.

Do

Since you've got new people mingling, provide some fun and games to help the process along. Lay out a Twister mat—the timeless excuse to get physical with a crush—in one corner and see if anyone takes up the suggestion. Or repurpose the classic autumn party game of hanging a bunch of apples (or donuts, if fruit sounds too healthy) by strings from the ceiling with a thumb tack or piece of putty; in this game, several pairs of contestants with their hands tied behind their backs race against each other to see who can eat theirs the fastest (if it falls to the floor, they're out!).

Ex Games

Another variation of this event: The Used-Date Party, made famous in an episode of *Sex and the City*. Each guest brings an ex they're no longer into but still think is a great person and wouldn't mind setting up with a friend. It's like recycling for relationships! Just be warned: This version can get a little dicey as old flames sometimes reignite when competition appears.

23 Nuts and Bolts Party

Want to throw a matchmaking party to be remembered? For this event, each of your guests gets a nut or bolt and spends the party trying to find the person who has the complementing piece. While it's great for large groups in which not everyone knows one another, it also works among friends as a fun excuse to hang out with someone you don't otherwise talk to very much. Your soulmate might just be the one holding the matching hardware—or one of the people you meet along the way to finding it.

Prep

Hit the hardware store and pick up a bunch of different pairs of bolts and their matching nuts (the round-ish piece with a hole in the center that screws onto the bolt). Get them out of mixed hardware bins to make sure they're all different sizes, or guests will have more than one match apiece. Aim to invite an equal number of male and female guests, and buy exactly half as many pairs as the number of guests coming (if you're not sure, get half as many as the number of invitees). At home, unscrew the pairs and put all the nuts in one bowl by the door and all the bolts in another.

Do

As they arrive, the guys should pick bolts and the girls should pick nuts. (You'll need to modify this somewhat for an LGBT crowd, but the basic idea is the same.) Tell them that their goal for the first half of the night is to try their bolt in all of the nuts or vice versa. If you end up with extra pieces leftover, let those who haven't found a match yet grab a few more and try again.

Partner Games

Keep the atmosphere light by offering these two games for newly coupled pairs to play.

Taboo. See how in sync matches are with this board game in which one partner has to get the other to guess a word on a card without using the top key clue words.

Baby If You Love Me, Won't You Please Smile? Do your best to crack up your match: One partner sits in a chair while the other attempts to make him or her smile using this signature phrase (and anything else he or she wants to say or do), while the seated partner replies—trying to stay straight-faced—"Baby I love you, but I just can't smile."

24 Truth or Dare Party

At thirteen or thirty, this game never gets old. It's always fun to learn new and naughty things about your friends, and to watch people do crazy and embarrassing stuff. But it can get even better, if you raise the stakes. This Valentine's Day, have a Truth or Dare party that is blown out into a massive, multiplayer competition complete with fake money. And because it's Valentine's Day, it's bound to inspire some sweet and smoochy dares!

Prep

You'll need to decide on a form of faux currency for guests to "buy" and "sell" truths and dares. Consider printing up your own money with a funny photo of you or a friend in place of the president and cleverly comic sayings where the "United States of America" and "In God We Trust" usually go. Or, go the easy route and use *Monopoly* money.

Do

Guests are given fake money and, throughout the night, walk around and pose the question "Truth or dare?" to other guests. If the person chooses truth, the asker asks them a question, and if it's answered honestly (any witnesses can help judge), the asker hands over a dollar. If the person chooses dare, the asker challenges them to do something difficult, outrageous, or silly. If he or she completes the dare, the asker gives them a dollar. In either case, if the person refuses, he or she has to give the *asker* a dollar. Feel free to negotiate higher pay rates for especially tough dares. (But set some ground rules for proposed dares, like nothing illegal, physically dangerous, or totally distasteful.) The person with the most dollars at the end of the night wins! Some guests will be aiming to rack up a wad of bucks; others will be happy to go broke just to instigate the most mayhem.

For prizes, you can give out gag gifts for first, second, and third place, or, cobble together your own trophy that the winner gets to keep—until you throw the party again next year and the champ is forced to defend his or her title.

Say Anything

It's hard to think of the perfect Valentine's Day truth or dare when you're on the spot. Here are a few ideas to get you started.

Truths

• Who's the hottest person you ever kissed? • What's the most embarrassing thing you ever did to get someone's attention? • If you had to choose between [name three guys or girls], who would you hook up with?

Dares

• Wear a sign on your back for the next hour that reads "Pinch Me." • Do your best cheerleader audition with your crush's name in place of the team name—at top volume, including at least one official jump. • Walk over to your crush and do the mating dance of the blue-footed booby (accuracy not required).

25 Anti-Valentine's Day Party

A woman by the name of Esther A. Howland created the first mass-produced valentines in the US in the 1840s. So if you're a member of the camp that believes Valentine's Day is a money-making invention of the greeting card companies—or you're just having a romantically challenged moment—you now know to whose estate you should address your hate mail. In the meantime, why not gather some fellow down-on-love friends and have a night of cathartic fun?

Prep

At the entrance, set up a table with nametags that have unlucky-in-love descriptions, like "Hello, My Name Is"… Bitter, Wandering Eye, or The Other Woman. Leave blank ones and pens for people who want to create their own. Display posters from romantic movies like *The Proposal*, *The Notebook*, and *Romeo + Juliet*, each one vandalized with a big red circle with a slash through it. Put out bowls of red roses cut up into pieces, and tape anti-love quotes on the walls.

Serve

Provide conversation hearts printed with anti-love sentiments—try Bittersweets from Despair.com. Or make your own heart-shaped cookie versions instead: Simply cut heart cookies in half with a jagged line before baking to represent broken hearts.

Do

If you're having a small group of close friends over, have everyone bring a photo of their evil ex or the crush who stupidly rejected them. Then have fun bashing the exes in the most creative way you can come up with: Supply Sharpies for blacking out teeth and adding devil horns, pin the faces on your old Raggedy Ann or Andy and use them as voodoo dolls; tape them onto an America's Least Wanted poster; or stick them to appropriate surfaces like the doormat, garbage can, and toilet bowl. Inviting a crowd? Set a rule of no kissing or hugging; offenders have to wear the scarlet letters—PDA (Think: lipstick on the arm or forehead, or red construction paper cut-outs pinned to clothing.) For a true emotional release, get a heart-shaped piñata for people to bash in, or play a romantic movie and hand out noisemakers so guests can boo and drown out the sappiest, most unrealistic moments.

Love Sucks Playlist

"Love Stinks" (The J. Geils Band) • "Already Gone" (Eagles) • "Love Bites" (Def Leppard) • "Goodbye to You" (Scandal) • "Goodbye Earl" (Dixie Chicks) • "U + Ur Hand" (P!nk) • "Potential Breakup Song" (Aly & AJ) • "Irreplaceable" (Beyoncé) • "Everything About You" (Ugly Kid Joe) • "Before He Cheats" (Carrie Underwood) • "Smile" (Lily Allen) • "Gives You Hell" (The All-American Rejects)

26 Sadie Hawkins Day Party

Sadie Hawkins Day gets its name from an old comic strip called *Li'l Abner*, which ran from 1934 to 1977. Sadie Hawkins was a girl from a hillbilly town who couldn't snag a husband. So her dad organized a race for all of the local unmarried girls to chase after the town's bachelors, and whoever they caught they could marry. This plotline became the inspiration for Sadie Hawkins Day dances across the country, in which girls had to invite guys to a dance instead of the other way around. Nowadays, girls often make the first move, but it's still fun to throw a party to give them an excuse!

Prep

Invite only girls, and on the invitation, explain that they need to ask a date to come with them. Of course, if someone shows up alone or with a friend, it's totally OK. But the point is to get as many girls to ask out guys as possible.

Wear

Some Sadie Hawkins parties are hillbilly-themed to match the setting and characters in the comic that invented them. If you want to go this route, tell everyone to come in farmer duds like overalls or denim cut-offs, gingham shirts, and straw hats (don't forget to complete the look by chewing on a piece of hay). Otherwise, just wear something fun and date-like.

Serve

If you're doing a hillbilly theme, label a big bowl of punch as "moonshine" or—more authentic to the comic strip—"kickapoo joy juice." You can also serve the usual Valentine's Day fare, like red and pink cookies and candy, or a big heart-shaped cake frosted white and decorated with little red cinnamon candies.

Girl Power Playlist

"One Way or Another" (Blondie) • "I Know What Boys Like" (The Waitresses) • "It's Raining Men" (The Weather Girls) • "Don't Cha" (Pussycat Dolls) • "Sooner or Later" (Madonna) • "The Boy Is Mine" (Brandy & Monica) • "Girlfriend" (Avril Lavigne) • "Milkshake" (Kelis) • "Fergalicious" (Fergie) • "Rude Boy" (Rihanna) • "I Do Not Hook Up" (Kelly Clarkson) • "The Tide Is High" (Blondie)

Do

The original Sadie Hawkins story was all about a girl using her strengths to chase down a reluctant guy, who then became hers for life. Play off that by slapping a pair of plastic handcuffs on each guest and the date she wrangled as they come through the door—he's hers for the night! Or, as soon as everyone's arrived, hold a mass mock-marriage ceremony for all the pairs; replace the usual vows with funny ones, like promising to "love, honor, obey, and refill her drink" until "death do us part—or midnight, whichever comes first."

27 Pre-Prom Cocktail and Photo Party

The prom isn't just a party, it's a rite of passage signifying the end of your high school days and the start of your adult social life. So, what does that mean? Learning how to throw a cocktail party! Keep it intimate and relaxed, and it'll be an event to remember—as well as a way to take some of your best photos of the evening.

Prep

Invite the friends with whom you plan to travel to the dance, as well as their parents, who will love the idea of giving their kids a proper send-off and may even stay to party after you leave.

If at all possible, schedule the gathering for the last hour before the sun goes down—photographers call this the "golden hour" because the warm light is the most flattering. Scout a location with the perfect backdrop, whether it's a stone wall or flowering tree, or the front stairs. Designate this as the photo spot for later on.

Serve

Prep a small table outside and cover it with a long tablecloth, a stack of cocktail napkins, and wine glasses or champagne flutes (plastic versions are OK). Serve both sparkling cider and bubbly since you'll have people who are underage and people who aren't. You'll need one bottle for every three guests, which gives each person two servings. Also, fill a clear glass pitcher with water, ice, and either cucumber or lemon slices, and put out separate glasses for it. Set out several small bowls of plain nuts and mints, and go with simple cheese and crackers unless your parents have offered to make fancier hors d'oeuvres (nothing messy, though!).

Photography Tips

For great group photos, have everyone stand at a 45-degree angle toward the center, and turn just their heads to the photographer. To take close-ups, press the "macro" button (it usually has a flower symbol on it), which will blur the background for a cool, professional-looking image.

Do

Once everyone's gotten a glass, ask the parents to make toasts. (Don't forget to take pictures of this!) Then, after some time spent socializing, call people's attention to the photo spot. Get shots of everyone together as well as just the girls and just the guys. Then rotate photographers so that everybody gets a shot with his or her parents and one alone with his or her date. Also, keep your digital camera in hand in between posed shots to capture little moments like your best friend kissing his girlfriend, or your date straightening his tie or smiling at her parents.

28 After-Prom Pajama Party

Prom is often an all-night event that continues on into the wee hours of the morning. When you're finished dancing, keep the night going by shedding your heels and constricting tuxes and bringing the party home. It could be the one time your parents green-light a co-ed slumber party, so seize the opportunity!

Wear

Be sure to tell your invitees that this is not just a sleepover but a true pajama party—their cutest PJs will be their "costume" for the event, long before it's time to actually crash. Help your guests accessorize by giving out personalized sleep masks as favors.

Prep

Cover your living room floor with blankets and pillows and as many stuffed animals as you can collect from friends and younger siblings. Go with a moon and stars theme for any paper products you pick up—you could even plaster your ceiling with little glow-in-the-dark star stickers for a cool lights-out surprise.

Serve

Put out "bedtime" milk and cookies at the start of the party, pizza or other snacks at 4 am, then a bright-and-early breakfast buffet in the morning with foods like scrambled eggs, pancakes, bacon, and home fries. Not really in a cooking mood at the crack of dawn? Go with ready-to-serve stuff instead like bagels and donuts.

Do

Try a version of Hide-and-Seek where one person hides and the rest search for him while wearing their sleeping masks. Or play Blind Man's Bluff—basically tag, but the person who's "it" (aka the "blind man") is blindfolded. Also check out the sleeping-bag clothes-swap game in the Ice-Breaker Party on page 86—even more fun in PJs. If all else fails ...pillow fight! Precut slits in old down pillows to make the feathers fly just like in the movies.

Anti-Lullaby Playlist

"No Sleep Till Brooklyn" (Beastie Boys) • "Talking In Your Sleep" (The Romantics) • "Enter Sandman" (Metallica) • "Morning Song" (Jewel) • "Dream On" (Aerosmith) • "Wake Me Up Before You Go-Go" (Wham!) • "Don't Dream It's Over" (Crowded House) • "Runnin' Down a Dream" (Tom Petty) • "Whose Bed Have Your Boots Been Under?" (Shania Twain)

PHOTO STATION

Create a jammies-oriented "under the covers" photo spot by hanging pillowcases and a blanket on the wall with removable plastic hooks from the drug store. Let guests crawl behind them while having someone snap a seemingly scandalous photo of them "in bed" together. The bed-on-the-wall trick makes it look like the camera's on the ceiling!

29 Alterna-Prom

Maybe you're just not into prom. After all, the wasteful spending on gowns and tuxes, the popularity contest of the prom king and queen, the top-40 bubblegum music, and the pressure to find a "perfect" date can all get kind of annoying. If you're feeling like the event is just another example of pointless conformity, show the prom committee a thing or two by throwing an alterna-prom instead.

Prep

Pick a date. You could make a strong anti-establishment statement by holding your party the same night as the school's, or hold it on a different date so that friends who want to can attend both. Hold it at your place if you have enough space; otherwise reserve the back room of a restaurant or ask to use a local hall like the American Legion.

Wear

Come up with a fun theme that captures your reason for throwing an alterna-prom. Here are a few ideas.

- **Recession Pricing.** Everyone's entire outfit must cost no more than $20.
- **Hot Mess.** Wear the tackiest, trashiest, most out-of-style suit or frock you can find.
- **Pretty in Pink.** Like Molly Ringwald's dress in the movie of the same name, everything you wear must be homemade or at least altered by you from its original store-bought state.

- **Fright Night Prom.** Come as an undead prom king, '70s horror queen Carrie, or any other doomed dancegoer from film or urban legend.
- **Dude Looks Like a Lady.** Girls wear the pants, boys wear the dresses—always a classic.
- **Dancing With Myself.** Everyone goes stag—no one is allowed to bring an official "date."

Do

Award homemade crowns and tiaras with unique royal titles, like Prom Queen of Originality, Prom Lord of the Dance, or Prom Prince of Paupers.

PHOTO STATION

Set up a classic, corny, prom-style photo station. Hang a solid-color sheet on the wall, then tie helium balloons together into an arc or place a big, cheap, fake floral arrangement on a table to one side of a banner with the name of your prom and the date. The juxtaposition of your alternative outfits and/or funny poses against the traditional backdrop makes for perfectly ironic souvenir shots.

Bottom 40

Rather than dancing all night to the overplayed hits of the day, have each guest bring music they love, but doubt that anyone else will have heard before, and play a mix of it at the party.

30 Fortune-Telling Party

From pretty much the beginning of time, every society has practiced some form of divination—that is, trying to figure out what's going to happen tomorrow before it actually does. The Ancient Greeks had a priestess doling out prophecies for gold at the Oracle of Delphi, and today people flock to places like Sedona, Arizona to connect with the supposed psychic energy there. So what does the future have in store for you and your friends? Med school? Cruise ship director? A life of petty crime? Forecast one another's destinies at this fortune-telling grad party.

Prep

You'll be predicting what's in the stars for your guests, so blanket the ceiling with tiny glow-in-the-dark stars or Christmas lights, and turn the regular lights down low. Put ambiance-enhancing elements on the coffee table like a deck of tarot cards, a crystal ball, and cool, illustrated books on astrology and dream interpretation (borrow them from the library if you don't want to buy them).

Serve

Fortune cookies! Also put out a bowl of apples along with a peeler and tell people to take off the skin in one curly strip: It's supposed to form the first letter of your future love's name when it hits the floor. For drinks, put out loose leaf tea along with Thermoses of hot water, cups, and a tea leaf-reading cheat sheet.

Steep a pinch of leaves in a cup with hot water; allow it to soak for a few minutes, drink the tea, and then look for shapes in the wet leaves left at the bottom of the cup. See a heart? Love may be near. See an elephant? You have good luck! (And perhaps a vivid imagination.)

Private Palm-Reading Booth

Assign one person to give palm-readings all night. Readings don't have to be accurate, just entertaining, so make it someone with a flair for the dramatic! Disguise the chosen palm reader in costume and station him or her inside a tent made of sheets draped over furniture, filled with pillows and electric candles.

Do

Here are a few more fortune-telling suggestions.

Runes. These are letters of an ancient Germanic alphabet, which some now use to answer questions about the future. The letters are written on small stones, which are spilled out of a bag at random. Those facing up are interpreted by the meaning assigned to each letter.

I Ching. Dating back to 1000 BC, the I Ching is an ancient Chinese practice that involves flipping coins to determine a pattern that, when interpreted according to a manual, helps answer a question asked.

Scrying. You gaze at something with a reflective surface—water, precious stones, polished metal, a crystal ball—and basically zone out until images symbolizing the future begin to appear.

31 Bonfire Party

There's something about a bonfire that puts people in an altered state of mind. Between the meditative flames and the idea of burning away the past, what could be a better symbol for a graduation party? Bring all your friends together for a warm night of sharing memories, casting off the concerns of the last four years, and looking forward to the future.

Prep

If you have a fire pit or chimenea in your back yard, you're all set. If not, hold your event at a beach (if fires are permitted), or at a campground by renting a site for the night. In all cases, you'll need dry wood (check the supermarket for precut bundles), kindling like dry twigs and newspaper, a lighter, and possibly a bottle of lighter fluid if you have any doubts about your fire-starting prowess. Don't forget some giant jugs of water to put the fire out.

Do

Tell everyone to bring one or more items that represent high school—whether it's the eight term papers they never want to think about again or the pair of soccer socks that lasted all four seasons since freshman year. (Steer clear of anything that could explode, shatter, or release toxic fumes, like plastic, rubber, glass, or alcohol.) Have each guest explain the significance of his or her items and then toss them into the fire as a way to say goodbye to the past few years.

You can also ask guests to bring a letter to their future selves describing how they feel about life right now, what their hopes and fears are, and where they want to be in 10 years. That night, put the letters into a time capsule that you'll bury (or just tuck away) and dig up for your ten-year high school reunion. Use a waterproof container (and/or bag everything inside in plastic zipper bags) and write the location in your yearbook so you don't forget.

Grad Party Playlist

"Kodachrome" (Simon & Garfunkel) • "My Old School" (Steely Dan) • "School's Out" (Alice Cooper) • "Another Brick in the Wall (Part 2)" (Pink Floyd) • "It's the End of the World As We Know It (And I Feel Fine)" (R.E.M.) • "Graduate" (Third Eye Blind) • "Graduation (Friends Forever)" (Vitamin C) • "Good Riddance (Time of Your Life)" (Green Day) • "The Last Song" (The All-American Rejects)

32 Grad Night Shut-In

Graduating from high school is monumental—so much so that people tend to go pretty crazy that night and can wind up in all kinds of places and in all kinds of messes. To prevent your graduation night from going amok, host a shut-in party that keeps people together all night. Your friends won't want to leave till the morning light—which is a good thing, since you won't let them!

Prep

Grad night should be a blowout, so try to get as many guests to come as you can. If you or a friend have a big house, great; if not, petition your school for use of a gymnasium or lunchroom (see Make It Official). Start the party soon after the school ceremony is over, and give a strict window for arrivals—say, between one and two hours later. The party should be the first and only party people go to that night—that's the point of a shut-in. When people arrive, have someone collect keys at the door from anyone who drove themselves; nobody gets them back till at least 9 am the next morning.

Do

Come up with a bunch of unique activities for your party. (Raise funds beforehand to pay for them, as needed.) Some ideas are a gladiator-style joust game; a bounce house; a dunk tank; a baseball speed pitch game; casino tables; the services of an airbrush tattoo artist; a Jell-O wrestling tournament (put Fun Jell in an inflatable kiddie pool); or tournaments of Rock Band, air hockey, ping pong, billiards, hoops, Wiffle ball, or darts. Announce an 11 pm game of flashlight tag, laser tag, or paintball. Hook up a karaoke machine at midnight. Schedule a 4 am movie showing when energy is bound to be dropping (check out Outdoor Movie Night, page 88, for creative screening setups). Finally, at 7 am, serve breakfast!

Make It Official

Parents' groups in some school districts organize "lock-in" parties like this one and call them Project Graduation. They seek donations from local businesses to cover the costs and hold the event at a venue like a health club, where students are bused right after the school ceremony. Instead of footing the bill for your party yourself, consider lobbying the PTA in your district (or maybe a few parents who own businesses) to form a Project Graduation committee. Communities like to throw down money for these events because they know it keeps kids from causing havoc in town!

33 Off-to-College Goodbye Party

Lots of people throw grad parties to commemorate high school in June. But at that point, you and your classmates still have all summer left to hang out with one another. The real life change comes in August when a lot of people head out for college and go their separate ways. That's when you truly need a gathering to say goodbye, so get everyone together and make it a send-off to remember.

Prep

If you or your friends have print photo albums from elementary school, junior high, and high school, have everyone bring them and put them out on the coffee table for guests to flip through. Or, collect everyone's favorite digital pictures beforehand and create a slide show set to music to play on your TV at the party.

Do

Make Yearbook Frames. Buy or make 8" x 10" photo mats (1" to 2"-thick borders that go around photos) for each guest. At the party, sign one another's mats with thin black markers or metallic silver ink pens. Then, have everyone pose for a group photo to commemorate the last time you were all together. Frame it with the signed mat and it'll serve as a reminder of home when you're all away at college.

Trade Postcards. Tell each guest to bring a bunch of stamped postcards addressed to themselves at their September addresses. On the way in, people will drop the postcards in a box by the door. On their way out, everyone reaches in and grabs as many as they brought, and then sends them out in the fall, ensuring handwritten mail for everyone!

Read Senior Wills. If you're inviting underclassmen, hold a reading of your fellow former seniors' last wills and testaments. Each guest departing for bigger and better things gets up and reads aloud the "items"—their back-row seat in study hall or their never-fail ability to sneak in after curfew undetected—they'd like to leave to their younger friends still stuck in high school.

Make a Send-Off Circle. Sit in a circle and have everyone tell their favorite story, or reveal their favorite quality, about each person in the group. To offer one another some parting words of wisdom, trade copies of a fill-in gift book like *Take Me With You: Off-to-College Advice From One Chick to Another*.

Farewell Fete Playlist

"We Gotta Get Out of This Place" (The Animals) • "Save Tonight" (Eagle-Eye Cherry) • "Never Say Goodbye" (Bon Jovi) • "Leaving on a Jet Plane" (Me Too and the Gimme Gimmes) • "Goodbye to You" (Michelle Branch) • "Hey There Delilah" (Plain White T's) • "Don't You (Forget About Me)" (Simple Minds) • "Landslide" (The Dixie Chicks) • "Photograph" (Nickelback)

34 Parlor Game Night

With no TV and not much to do at night but gossip and sip tea in the parlor, the Victorians were the ones to popularize many of the party games that we know today. Some games involved small props, others required nothing but the players themselves. Take a cue from them and host your own night of friendly competition!

Prep

Simply choose a date and choose the games! For more fun, make it a monthly get-together hosted by a different person each time.

Serve

The host should supply the munchies, which can range from gourmet delivery to convenience-store snacks. It's all good!

Do

Here are a few great parlor games to get you started.

Celebrity. Everyone writes down names of famous people and puts them in a bowl. Each guest picks a name and can say and do anything he wants to get the group to guess it. After you've gone through every name in the bowl, put them back in and start round two, which is played just like regular charades. For round three, use the same names once again, but this time, the presenter is only allowed to say a single word.

Wink. Everyone sits in pairs in a two-row semicircle on the floor, one partner sitting in front of the other. One person ("the wink") sits in the center of the semicircle. The wink calls up some of the front-row players by naming a category (for example, "everyone with bangs"). Each of them races to be the first to kiss the wink (who can't move), while each of their partners tries to restrain them. The winner becomes the new wink. The old wink takes the winner's former spot. Those called who didn't win switch places with their partner.

Mafia. One person acts as narrator. Ideally, ten other players draw slips of paper to determine who's a mafia member (three people), townsperson (six people), and nurse (one person). During the first phase, called "night," everyone closes their eyes, then the mafia open theirs and silently agree on a player to "kill." The narrator then tells the mafia to "go to sleep" and "wakes" the nurse, who chooses one person to save. The narrator announces "daytime," and everyone opens their eyes. The narrator announces who has been "murdered" (or that no murder has taken place, if the nurse saved the right person) and the group must try to ID one mobster to execute. Once put to death, the person reveals their true role. Play continues between day and night until all mafia are dead—or they outnumber the townspeople.

35 Ultimate Scavenger Hunt

If you've ever wondered how the scavenger hunt got started, it was all the idea of a 1930s high society event planner named Elsa Maxwell. Originally from Iowa, Elsa left school at 14 to travel, met a ton of glamorous people, and eventually became the premier party hostess of her time. The premise of the Scavenger Hunt is simple: Whoever finds the most items on a list the fastest wins a prize. Today, the event has become a high school and college classic that often entails behavior that is anything but high society!

Prep

Invite as many people as possible (like the whole school!)—the bigger the group, the better the competition. Also decide whether it'll be a walking or driving scavenger hunt. It doesn't matter, as long as everyone uses the same mode of transportation (feet or wheels). If you need help organizing it, enlist a friend to be the co-host. You can come up with the list of items and promote the event together.

You'll need a home base—a place where you start and end up. For a small group, your house or apartment is fine. For a big crowd, make it a park, playground, driveway or empty parking lot. Be sure that there's music and snacks.

Do

As people arrive, collect a small entry fee from each team to help cover the cost of prizes, which could either be the money itself or small, funny gag gifts. If you're driving, one car equals one team. If you're walking, set a size limit—say, five people per team. Right before go-time, get up on the roof of a car (or park bench) and announce the main rules.

1) All teams must return by X o'clock, and the team with the most points wins. For ties, the team who comes back the earliest wins.

2) No speeding, trespassing, stealing, bodily endangerment, or law-breaking of any other kind in the pursuit of items.

After that, hand out the checklist and give 'em an "on your mark, get set, go!" The hosts stay put to mind the fort. When everyone's back, resume the party and let everyone swap stories while you count the loot. In addition to rewarding the overall winner, give out an honorable mention for the funniest objects collected (like if there's a "baby carrot" on the list and someone brings back their baby sister wearing a carrot costume.).

Some Ideas for Huntables

The more creative the items on your checklist, the more fun the hunt will be. Here are a few ideas to get you started.

• photo (digital or print) of someone kissing a police officer • stamped, postmarked postcard from out of state • a cheerleader in uniform • signature of Flo, the graveyard shift waitress at the local truck stop diner • one extra-large size condom

36 Trivial Pursuit Party: Friends Edition

The iconic trivia board game—invented back in 1979 by two bored Canadian buddies —has spawned more than 50 different editions, from Country Music to Totally '80s. But there's room for one more. Test your friends' memory, loyalty, and group dedication by quizzing them on what's really important: one another!

Prep

It's best to make this a get-together with a small group of people who know one another well. Before the party, you'll need to create the game. First, come up with six trivia categories. You could use the standard Trivial Pursuit categories like Geography (questions about where you had your first kiss or last fender bender), History (facts about your childhood), and Sports and Leisure (questions on favorite pastimes). Or create your own, like Inside Jokes, Romantic History, and Pet Peeves.

Then, ask each friend to take five index cards, and put one question about himself or herself from each category on each card. (Answers are listed the same way, but on the back.) Assign each of the categories one of the colors on a standard Trivial Pursuit board: blue, pink, green, orange, yellow, and brown. Have everyone dot the right color next to each question. The host should make cards, too. Collect the cards (no peaking!) when your friends arrive.

Do

Take the board and pie pieces from any edition of regular Trivial Pursuit. Play is exactly the same—you roll the die, move your pie, and try to earn all six wedges by answering questions correctly. If someone reading a question to another player sees that it's about that player, the reader must put the card back and pick another.

Play Jeopardy-Style

You can also use these questions in a game of Jeopardy. Questions can be worth 100–1,000 points, depending on how hard you think they are, and whoever gets the most points, wins. For this game, all you need is a scorecard—no board, pieces, or Alex Trebek necessary.

37 Ice-Breaker Party

When you're starting off with a new group—like the crew at your new summer job or camp, or your college or boarding school freshman hall—people tend to be on their best (read: boring) behavior until something breaks the ice. So be the hero and invite everyone over for some games designed to bring people out of their shells. Or just play them to get even closer (literally, in some cases!) to your current friends.

Do

There are three basic ways to make people feel more comfortable together: learn about one another, break the touch barrier, and/or act like idiots together. Here are some great games to get your started.

Revealing Games

I Never. Sit in a circle. One person says "Never have I ever..." and completes the sentence with something they've never done, like "been abroad" or "gone skinny-dipping." Anyone who has done that thing has to do an agreed-upon action, like eat something spicy or put fifty cents toward a pizza for the group.

Whose Story Is It? Send three people to the front of the room at a time. Each one writes down an outrageous but true fact or story about themselves. Shuffle them, pick one, and read it aloud, and the crowd then gets to ask the three people three questions each to try and determine whose story it was. (The storywriters all reply as if it was their story.) The crowd then decides whose story it was—and that person wins, even if it wasn't really theirs.

Touchy-Feely Games

Suck and Blow. In this game made famous by the movie *Clueless*, pass a playing card around a circle by placing it on your lips and sucking inward to hold it in place, then pressing it against the lips of the person next to you and blowing to release it. Drop it and you're both out—but your consolation prize is a kiss!

Kiss or Dare. In this combo of two classics, you spin a bottle in the center of the circle and whomever it lands on gets to choose what they want from you: a kiss or a dare.

Action Games

Thumper. Each player comes up with a funny hand gesture and shows everyone what it is. To start, one player does his own gesture plus another person's of his choice, then that person does their own gesture plus someone else's, and so on. If it's your turn and you blank on what gesture to do next, everyone has to start again.

Clothes Swap. Two boy/girl teams jump into a pair of sleeping bags, strip out of their clothes, and put on their partner's, racing to see which couple can swap outfits the fastest.

38 Outdoor Movie Night

The drive-in theaters of the 1950s had the right idea by bringing great movies to the great outdoors. The only thing lacking: a little extra legroom. Cities across the country have solved that problem by swapping bucket seats for blankets and hosting al fresco film screenings in public parks. But why wait for a town-sponsored event? Whether it's on your back lawn or a city rooftop, an outdoor movie night makes a great summer party.

Prep

One option is to simply position your regular TV in an open window or sliding door—of course that requires windows in the right place and height to allow people to see from a deck or backyard (you'll also need an extension cord and a long cable). Otherwise, you'll need a projector (rent one online or at a local audio-visual rental place, or ask around to see if anyone you know will lend theirs out) as well as a DVD player (like the one in your laptop), speakers (like the ones you use for your MP3 player), and a screen. You can buy or rent a tripod-style screen or just show your movie on a white sheet on the side of your house. The image might be slightly lower quality, but the event will be just as fun. Tell everyone to bring a sleeping bag and pillow and spread them out in front of the screen. You could also pull over any lounge or lawn chairs you have, or even haul an old couch out there.

Serve

This one's a no-brainer: Get your microwave working on some popcorn, at least one bag per guest. For extra authentic appeal, order a carton of old-school, red-and-white popcorn boxes online. (If you really feel like going all out, party rental companies will rent you a carnival-style popcorn maker for the night.) Round out the menu with canned sodas and boxed movie theater candy.

The Real Thing

In the 1950s, there were more than 4,000 drive-ins across the US, but today there are fewer than 400 left! If you have friends with cars, keep the nostalgia alive by setting up a screen in your driveway and making it a true drive-in! These movies are great picks because they feature actual scenes with drive-ins.

Grease (1978) • *The Outsiders* (1983) • *Spies Like Us* (1985) • *Twister* (1996)

39 Sleepaway Camp Party

Campfire songs, arts and crafts, color wars, bunk raids, and making out at Inspiration Point—sleepaway camp has been one of the great American traditions for over a century. Whether you're a die-hard camper or counselor in withdrawal, or a sleepaway virgin wanting to get in on the fun, throw this campy camp-themed party to get your Kumbaya fix!

Prep

The ideal spot for this party is a backyard with a fire pit, but you can create the same feel inside an apartment by setting up some fake Christmas trees and laying out some sleeping bags. Decorate your front door or the door to the backyard with a sign reading "Welcome to Camp ___," filling in the blank with a funny, fitting made-up name like "Camp Run-A-Mok." Instead of writing it out, wood-glue twigs to poster board in the shape of the letters. Make another sign with an arrow for Inspiration Point; the spot it points to can be just a secluded patch of trees or a room inside your house.

Serve

Over your fire pit or on your indoor stove, cook hot dogs (or veggie dogs) and make s'mores. Wash it all down with a jug of punch labeled "Bug Juice."

Do

As each person arrives, assign them a "bunk number." Create something to hand out with the number on it, like a Lincoln Log, a lanyard, or a cabin shape cut out of brown construction paper. Try and put the same number of people in each group, and then have each group come up with a skit, song, or random, ridiculous talent to perform at the mini Camp Talent Show at the end of the night. Or, announce that each cabin must come up with a way to prank another cabin by the end of the night, with the best prank winning bragging rights.

CAMP RUNAMOK

For more activities, go for the summer camp staples: arts and crafts and archery! Set up a craft table off to one side with materials for plastic lanyards or embroidery-thread friendship bracelets. Find an archery game for your Wii, or hang a bullseye on a tree and shoot at it from afar with suction arrows or novelty bows that shoot things like mini marshmallows instead of arrows.

Never been to camp?

Tragic! Get the scoop on what you're missing—and some party fodder—from these classic flicks.

Meatballs (1979) • *Little Darlings* (1980) • *Friday the 13th* (1980) • *Heavyweights* (1995) • *Wet Hot American Summer* (2001) • *Camp* (2003)

40 South Beach Pool Party

When it comes to America's best party spots, Miami's South Beach neighborhood ranks high on the list. With white sand beaches, sparkling art deco hotel pools, lively Latin culture, and legendary nightclubs, it has a rep for being the destination for world-class partiers. If you're lucky enough to have a pool, recreate your own South Beach with a glammed-up after-dark soiree using the water as the centerpiece.

Prep

Turn the pool lights on, but not the floodlights—use candles or lanterns to illuminate the rest of the party area, so that the water glows in the darkness. If you do use overhead lights, switch out the plain bulbs for colored ones. To mimic the neon hotel and club marquees on South Beach's main strip, Ocean Drive, get some candy-colored rope lights (the kind enclosed in a tube to create a solid band of light, rather than individual bulbs on a string like Christmas lights), and line the fence or tables with them, mark out a dance floor, or even twist them into big letters spelling out South Beach's nickname, SoBe. Set the arrival time right around sunset.

Serve

Set up a table for frozen drinks with a blender, glasses (fancy-shaped ones if you have them), spoons, straws, maraschino cherries, ice, and bottles of nonalcoholic daiquiri and piña colada mixes. Miami's culture is heavily influenced by its many Cuban immigrants, so serve staples like finger-size Cuban sandwiches (ham, roasted pork, Swiss cheese, pickles, and mustard on Cuban bread, pressed like a Panini), plantain chips, and tres leches cake.

Wear

Be sure everyone knows to come dressed to impress, rather than in the usual pool-party shorts and tees. It probably won't be long until someone winds up in the pool—fully clothed!

SoBe Playlist

"Miami" (Will Smith) • "Bailamos" (Enrique Iglesias) • "Rhythm Is Gonna Get You" • (Gloria Estefan & Miami Sound Machine) • "I Know You Want Me" (Pitbull) • "Kissed By the Sun" (John Beltran) • "I'm in Miami Trick" (LMFAO)

41 Meteor Shower Viewing Party

Every year around August 12, the sky is set ablaze with hundreds of shooting stars during the annual Perseids meteor shower. This awesome display occurs because the earth's orbit sends it straight through a cloud of dust particles, called meteoroids, which are flaking off of the Swift-Tuttle comet; when they hit our atmosphere, they burst into streaks of light. Viewing is best done far away from brightly lit cities, so head out to someone's house in the sticks for a screening of the planet's natural fireworks show.

Prep

Go to Nasa.gov to find out which night is expected to be the best for the Perseids this year. The most shooting stars fly by in the hours just before daybreak, when you can see up to 50 or more per hour, so set the start time of your party for 12 am. (This is one night you'll have to ask for an extended curfew!)

Turn off all outdoor lights. Arrange reclining lounge chairs in a circle with the heads together in the yard, or lay out sleeping bags right on the grass.

Serve

Place a small side table with drinks and munchies out on the lawn. Also, stock your fridge with the ingredients to cook up a big, hot breakfast at dawn! Garnish plates or orange juice glasses with sliced starfruit.

Do

Put on some tunes, lie back, and get ready to start making wishes! There's likely to be some lag time from one meteor to the next, so in between, try to locate constellations—you could even get a green laser pointer to point them out.

Another way to fill time in the dark: Play games that don't require light, getting up out of a supine position, or even looking at one another. Here are two to start you off.

Mr. Wizard. Assign four people to be Mr. Wizard. Everyone else asks "him" a question—something totally random, or of great (and comic) significance to your group. The first person who's part of the wizard gives the first word of an answer, the next person adds a word to continue the sentence, and so on, looping back around through all four people until one of them decides to end it by saying "period." Hilarious and oddly addictive!

Thumper. Check out the rules for this one in the Ice-Breaker Party on page 86. Instead of using gestures, make everyone's "sign" a funny sound instead. See how long you can go before the whole game dissolves into laughter.

42 Fourth of July Party

Fireworks, barbecues, tricolored flags with stripes and stars—Independence Day is one of the few holidays everyone in the US celebrates, regardless of religion or ethnicity. It's our most patriotic holiday, as it marks the anniversary of the signing of the Declaration of Independence back in 1776. And, best of all, it's also a sure signal of the beginning of summer! Get all of your pals together to celebrate with a star-spangled day of fun.

Prep

In your backyard or at a nearby park, lay out a tablecloth along with plates, cups, and silverware with a color palette of red, white, and blue. Weight the tablecloth down at each corner with a vase, candleholder, or mini metal bucket filled with sand and an American flag stuck in the center. Hang ribbons in the patriotic colors from tree branches encircling the party space as streamers.

Serve

Make mini sandwiches by layering cream cheese and strawberry jelly between white bread, cutting out star-shapes with a cookie-cutter, then skewering them with a toothpick garnished with a blueberry. For drink chillers, fill an ice tray with water, place a blueberry or raspberry in each compartment, and freeze, then drop the cubes into glasses of clear soda, like lemon-lime. For dessert, bake up a red velvet cake in a 13" x 9" pan, ice it with whipped topping or white frosting, and decorate the top with a square of blueberries in the upper left corner and stripes of strawberry slices arranged to look like the American flag.

Do

If you're handing out sparklers, keep your camera ready to get some cool shots. Turn off any outdoor lights, and set your camera on a low-light/no-flash mode to a slow shutter speed to capture trails of illumination as your subjects wave their sparklers. Rest your camera on a tripod or other flat surface while snapping shots to avoid blurriness.

Patriotic Playlist

"American Pie" (Don McLean) • "Volunteers" (Jefferson Airplane) • "American Girls" (Counting Crows) • "Kids in America" (The Muffs) • "American Music" (Violent Femmes) • "California Girls" (The Beach Boys) • "City of New Orleans" (Arlo Guthrie) • "America, F*** Yeah" (Team America) • "American Idiot" (Green Day) • "Young Americans" (David Bowie)

Fourth of July parties often have fireworks, but not always; at-home fireworks (including sparklers!) are actually prohibited or restricted in a number of states. Find out what's legal where you live at Firework-safety.com. And no matter where you live, it's dangerous to craft your own flammables (close to 10,000 people a year go to the hospital for firework-related injuries, usually from the homemade and/or illegal ones). So, be careful!

43 Desert Island Party

In real life, getting shipwrecked on a desert island would be a disaster. You'd have the mother of all sunburns and sand in crevices you didn't know you had. And good luck if you don't love seafood. The island you create for your party, on the other hand, will be a place where everyone will *want* to be stranded!

Prep

Every good desert island party should have surf and turf. That could mean a backyard pool and a deck covered in six inches of sand (you can buy cheap sandbox sand at home improvement stores—just prepare yourself for the cleanup!). In the city? Create a beach either in a park or on a rooftop with two kiddie pools, one filled with water and the other sand.

Three Things

Have people bring the three albums or foods they would want to have if stranded on a desert island. Then, play the music all night or eat the foods!

Once you've got all that squared away, decide if you want to do a theme within a theme: Your island could be the one frolicked on by Jack and Sawyer (from *Lost*), Ginger and Mary Ann (from *Gilligan's Island*), Kamehameha (the first King of Hawaii), or Jeff Probst and the competitors on *Survivor*.

Here are a few ideas.

Lost. Download and print out the Dharma Initiative logo, photocopy it, and glue-stick it to all your paper cups, plates, bags of chips, and soda bottles. Sit a stuffed polar bear somewhere prominent.

Gilligan's Island. Get everyone to come dressed as one of the characters. Use a permanent marker to write "S.S. Minnow" on a bunch of cheap toy boats and set them afloat in the pool. Make a "coconut radio" by covering your speakers in natural-looking materials like bamboo placemats with a few twigs stuck in for good measure.

Survivor. Designate an immunity idol (an old troll doll or a souvenir figurine) and set up challenges to run throughout the night—underwater handstand contest, chicken fights, or a tricycle race around the pool.

Luau. At this classic Hawaiian party, be sure to include "hula" hoops, grass skirts, coconut bras, and a *lei* for each guest as they arrive. Serve virgin piña coladas and coconut cream pie, and play beachy tunes like Israel Kamakawiwo'ole's "Somewhere Over the Rainbow," and The Beach Boys' "Kokomo."

44 Blackout Party

There's something about a blackout that invokes a sense of mystery and playfulness in a group of people. But you don't have to wait for the next storm to try and navigate your way through a dark room with friends. At this dance party, stage your very own blackout (several of them, in fact). You won't be quite sure whom you're dancing with, and that's half the fun!

Prep

Hold the party in a room with as few windows as possible, like a basement. Use cardboard, black sheets, or both to cover what windows there are and block out any outside light. Push all the furniture to the sides of the room for more dance space (and fewer tripping hazards). Buy a bunch of dollar-store keychain flashlights to give out to guests as they arrive, or ask them to bring their own (but they have to be those really small ones). Plug in a nightlight by the exit for safety during the party.

Unplugged Playlist

"Dance in the Dark" (Lady Gaga) • "Electric Feel" (MGMT) • "Black" (Pearl Jam) • "Electric City" (The Black Eyed Peas) • "Lights Out" (Fabolous) • "Electric Avenue" (Eddy Grant) • "Electricity" (Moby) • "Blinded By the Light" (Manfred Mann's Earth Band)

Wear

Tell everyone to wear all black and only black. The darker the clothes, the less visible people will be when the lights go out.

Do

The party starts with the lights on. Then, every third song or so, hit the light switch for a blackout song. (See blackout song suggestions in sidebar). People are free to flick on their flashlights for an impromptu light show, or just groove in the dark with a mystery dance partner!

Off the Grid

Have a real power outage? Throw an impromptu real blackout party. Though you won't have the electricity needed to play music on speakers, you can create a silent, candlelit rave. Grab some friends from the neighborhood (call them if the phone works, or ring their bells if they live nearby). Tell everyone to bring their own iPods (which are hopefully charged!) and rock out together with ear buds on, all to the same song or each to the beat of his own drummer. When you get hungry, hold a competition to see who can create the tastiest no-cook dish using up at least three perishable items from the fridge or freezer before they thaw.

45 Classic Dinner Party

Are you a budding chef who can't get your little brother to appreciate your killer fish tacos? Or perhaps you're just looking for a chance to try your hand at something beyond cereal? Invite over a group of friends and blow them away with your culinary genius.

Prep

Make a game plan for your dinner. This means calculating how long each dish takes to prepare and cook, then counting backward from dinner time to figure out in what order and at what precise time you need to start preparing each one. A game plan ensures that each dish will be ready at the same time (so that your peas aren't getting cold while your potatoes are still simmering), and that you'll actually be able to eat with your guests rather than be stuck in the kitchen all night.

Before you start cooking, practice *mise en place*. This French culinary term means having each of your ingredients chopped, peeled, grated, and measured out ahead of time. Another time-saver: Choose one or more dishes that can be prepared entirely the night before, then heated up (or served room temperature) at go-time.

Decorate your table with a centerpiece and other decorative touches, and make a mix of mellow ballads and instrumental music to play at low volume in the background.

Serve

Make at least two courses (like main entrée and dessert) and no more than four (those two, plus appetizer and soup). As you come up with a menu, think of what ingredients are in season and use them in your recipes. For example, strawberries and blueberries for summer, and pumpkin in autumn. Next, make sure there is variety in flavor, color, and texture. If you're serving cheese as an appetizer, leave it out of your main course. If your meat is a delicious caramel brown, add brightly colored side dishes, like a vegetable dish featuring red bell peppers or cherry tomatoes. Going with creamy-smooth mashed potatoes as your starch? Choose something crunchy like asparagus as your veggie.

Moveable Feast

You can also make it a "progressive" dinner party, where you move from house to house throughout the night. Start at your house where you'll serve the appetizers. Then go to one of your guest's places, where he'll serve the main course, and then to another friend's for dessert.

Do

Eat! And use the party as an opportunity to really converse with people. That means no texting or emailing from your cell during dinner!

46 The Perfect Picnic

Historians aren't exactly sure where or how the picnic first originated. The Japanese have a long history of eating outdoors, especially when the cherry trees are in bloom. In Victorian England, picnics were known to be elaborate affairs with tables and linens and china and servants! Whether you want your picnic to be a small affair or an all-out extravaganza, here's how to class up your al fresco dining event.

Prep

Pick a nearby park with lots of green grass. Take a blanket (an older quilt will do, plus a tarp for underneath if the grass is wet) and your spread. True picnic "baskets" have their charm, but newer backpack versions are made with thermal compartments that you can load with ice packs to keep perishables and sodas cool longer. You'll also need cutlery and dishes; see Keep It Eco-Friendly for suggestions for these.

Serve

A great picnic starts with a great spread. One classic example is a cheese platter with several different kinds of crackers, French bread, pepperoni, apples, pears, and honey—the salty and sweet tastes complement each other perfectly. Get small portions of several different kinds of cheese: one popular type like cheddar for neophytes, one spreadable option, like brie, and one that's tangy and hard, like a wedge of parmesan. If you slice the apples and pears ahead of time, spray them with lemon juice to keep them from browning. At the park, lay it all out on a large wooden cutting board along with a small knife for each cheese, a tiny spoon for the honey, and plenty of napkins. Ask friends to round out the meal by bringing cookies or brownies for dessert.

One more picnic staple that's simply a must: watermelon! Make yours a showstopper by carving the whole melon itself into the shape of a basket and serving a fruit salad inside. (Look online to find instructions about how to do this). Use berries, grapes, watermelon balls (from the portion you've scooped out), and any other fruit you want.

Do

You can only eat for so long, so have some activities on the agenda. Lawn games are perfect for a picnic. Some options: croquet, horseshoes, bocce ball, lawn bowling, Frisbee, box hockey, or the ever-popular and especially low-budget watermelon seed-spitting contest.

Keep It Eco-Friendly

Make your picnic truly green by using washable plates, forks, knives, and spoons, instead of their disposable counterparts. For cups, grab some of the stackable hard plastic ones. And use cloth napkins that can be thrown in the washing machine afterward—you can get these cheap from a secondhand store or make them yourself from old fabric.

47 Top Chef Cook-Off

On Bravo's hit reality competition *Top Chef*, "cheftestants" race to outdo one another in challenges like Breakfast in Bed, the Perfect Steak, or Healthy School Lunches, while the lucky judges get to sample delectable, creative variations on each dish. Play an amateur version at home, competing with your friends to create the freshest spin on a favorite food.

Prep

Base the party around a specific dish that your friends can elaborate on with special fixings and flavorings. For example, throw a Build-the-Best-Burger night where everyone has to make a specialty hamburger. Provide the ground meat, a few different kinds of breads or rolls, a ton of veggies, and access to every sauce in your fridge, plus whatever is in your herb and spice rack.

Another option: Pasta Perfection, where you supply plain canned tomato and cream sauces, an array of cheeses, veggies, spices, and some funky-shaped noodles, like gigli, a conelike flower shape, or croxetti, medallions imprinted with little pictures like a sailboat or a coat of arms.

Other foods that would work well as your backdrop for innovation are pancakes, brownies, and Rice Krispie treats. (Find a few more ideas in Stone Soup Soiree on page 110.)

Do

Make sure everyone has a small station in which to work, and assign them a number or code name to prevent biased judging. If you have a lot of guests (or if you think pairs would be more fun), split into teams. Set an alarm for the time you want to allot to prepping and cooking; say, 60 minutes. Then plate your dishes, tag them with their code name or number, and present them to the judges. These could be your parents, siblings, or significant others—anyone who didn't cook. Ask the judges to rate the creations based on taste (1–10 points), presentation (1–5 points), and originality (1–5 points). The champ gets the coveted title of Top Chef.

After the competition is over, everyone gets to eat! Remember to store whatever food is left over at the end—or, if it's unopened, donate it to a local food bank.

Peanut and Pickle Blintzes?

To keep things interesting, don't just put out standard ingredients. Throw in a few totally wacky decoy items—like turkey jerky, pickled eggs, and mini marshmallows. These ingredients might throw a team off course, or turn out to be surprise hits. Either way, a mixed bag will require people to think a little more, proving their culinary prowess.

48 Fondue Party

The word "fondue" comes from the French word *fondre*, meaning "to melt." It's a dish where you dip bread, meat, or fruit into a melted pot of things like cheese or chocolate. The tradition began in the mountains of Europe in the 18th century, when the Swiss would make stale bread and hardened cheese edible by heating up the cheese with white wine, and dipping the bread into the gooey mix. Fondue later became a disco-era dinner party fad, and today it's still a favorite for communal dining on a chilly winter night. There are even entire restaurants dedicated to the love of the melting pot.

Prep

The first thing you'll need is a fondue pot. There are two basic types: One uses alcohol or butane to fuel a little flame underneath the pot; the other is electrical and simply plugs into an outlet like a toaster. See if your parents or any of their friends have one. Be sure to read the included instructions carefully to avoid burns. All pots typically come with eight long, skinny forks for dipping, so invite accordingly.

Serve

Pick your fondue and your dippers. Here are some suggestions.

Cheese Fondue. Combine 3 tablespoons of all-purpose flour, 2 teaspoons dry mustard, 2 cups milk, 6 cups shredded sharp cheddar cheese, 1 teaspoon Worcester sauce, and 2 drops hot pepper sauce in your fondue pot. Use bite-size pieces of crusty bread, pepperoni, apples, carrots, peppers, or broccoli as dippers.

Dessert Fondue. Combine two packages of chocolate chips and one cup of heavy cream. You can also incorporate caramel, vanilla extract, white chocolate, peanut butter, or mint—when it comes to dessert, the possibilities are endless! Use angel food cake, pretzel rods, Biscotti or shortbread cookies, brownies, marshmallows, cherries, bananas, strawberries, or popcorn as dippers.

Go Retro

Pay homage to the fondue parties of the 1970s by blowing yours out into a full-on groove fest. Tell everyone to come in disco fashions (bell bottoms, loud flower patterns, halter dresses) and play tunes straight out of *Saturday Night Fever*. Hang a disco ball from the kitchen or dining room ceiling, turn down the lights, and get your dip on!

Do

Keep an eye on the pot; you'll probably need to stir the pot and adjust the temperature up and down a bit at times to keep it warm, but not scorching. Even if the top doesn't look or feel hot, the mixture on the bottom (closest to the flame) might be burning. Be on the lookout for floaters, too: According to one tradition, if you drop a piece of food into the pot, you have to kiss the person on your left; another tradition says you have to kiss everyone at the table. Make up your own rule about what happens when someone loses a chunk in the pot. And remember, no double-dipping!

49 Stone Soup Soiree

You won't actually be eating soup full of pebbles at this party. The concept of Stone Soup comes from an old fable in which a couple of hungry travelers tell some poor villagers that they can make a delicious soup out of just water and a rock, if only the villagers would be willing to donate a few odds and ends—like onions, carrots, potatoes, flour, herbs, and spices. Of course, those odds and ends are really all that's needed for a soup, and an hour later, everyone's enjoying a mouthwatering stew made from "just" a stone and some garnishes. Borrow this concept for a fun, creative feast where everyone contributes an ingredient to make a one-of-a-kind meal.

Prep

Decide what dish you want to base your party around. The concept works best with popular meals or desserts that are made by adding any number of optional elements—which your guests will bring—to a common base that you'll provide. For example, supply several store-bought or homemade pizza crusts and your grandma's famous sauce, and tell your friends to each bring a special type of cheese or topping. The more out-there the extras, the better: Instead of just plain old pepperoni, tell people to try to top one another on creativity points with stuff like blue cheese, pickles, or grapes. Some other dishes that are ripe for experimentation: baked potatoes, mac-and-cheese, tortillas, crepes, sandwiches, and salads.

Another option is to make it a just-desserts party with an ice cream sundae bar. You provide a couple half-gallons of vanilla and chocolate, and your friends try to outdo each other with crazy but delicious toppings like mini pretzels, jam, spiced nuts, maple syrup, or warm molasses cookies (those last two are fantastic together, by the way).

Do

Lay out a bunch of bowls for all of the various ingredients your guests bring to the table. Have everyone make their own combination with a small portion of the food (for instance, if you're making pizza, give each person a slice to create). Take pictures of each creation, name them, sample them, and vote on what came out the best. Your ingredient combo may sound weird at first, but it might just be the next Hawaiian pizza or Chubby Hubby ice cream!

Multi-Culti Cuisine

Can't think past pepperoni? Here are some of the crazy toppings popular on pizza around the world.

Japan: squid • Brazil: peas • Russia: red herring • India: mutton (sheep) • Costa Rica: coconut

50 Tasting Party

Wine has always had a cult following of aficionados who enjoy sampling and discussing the various varieties, but now people throw tasting parties for anything and everything. Tasting parties help people to become connoisseurs who can pick up on subtle distinctions between different flavors—and they're also a great excuse to spend a night stuffing your face with your favorite food!

Prep

Choose a type of food or drink to taste. Try to pick something that comes in lots of varieties and tastes different depending on the region it's from or the way it's made.

For example, coffee beans get their individual flavors from the places they're grown—like the Blue Mountains of Jamaica or the fields of Kona in Hawaii—and from the ways they're stored and roasted. Chocolate is differentiated by the origin of the cocoa (or *cacao*) beans used, and the actual percentage of cocoa in the recipe. Cheeses differ based on the animal the milk comes from (cow, sheep, or goat), and how it's aged and ripened. And barbecue sauce recipes vary by flavor—sweet or savory—and by region, from Kansas City to Memphis.

Once you've chosen a food, head to a specialty or gourmet store and pick up six to twelve varieties of it. For quantities, remember that you'll be trying a few sips or bites of each, so no need to get a full serving of every type for every person. If you want to turn the party into more of a meal at some point, pick up accompaniments as well, like cream and sugar for coffee, and crackers and fruit slices for cheese.

Do

Once you've laid out your smorgasbord, go through each variety one at a time. Have each guest take a taste and then come up with a few words to describe it, or agree or disagree with what someone else has said. Water and crackers can be used to help cleanse the palette between samplings.

Beyond "Yum"

Wine lovers discuss different vintages based on factors like "entry" (how it tastes as it first hits your mouth) and "finish" (how it tastes right after swallowing), and "length" (how long the flavor lasts). Some words they use to describe flavors are "closed" (little to no flavor or aroma), "confected" (overly candy-sweet), and "dry" (not sweet).

If your crowd is filled with connoisseurs, do a blind tasting to test how much they really know. Code all of the samples by number (only you have a master list of what's what) and have each guest write down what they think they're eating (brie? Camembert? Gorgonzola?). See who gets the most answers right! Or, hold a different kind of competition by having each guest bring one of the samples and voting on the best ones.

51 Ice Age Party

Only a mere 20,000 years ago, North America was frozen solid for a period of time that's known as the Ice Age. But it probably wasn't the first Ice Age, and it may not be the last, according to many scientists. So, bring on the next big chill a little early at your very own Ice Age party, where you'll create a cave in which you and your guests can huddle together for warmth (or just for fun)!

Prep

Create your cave by covering the walls with crinkled brown paper (buy a roll at an office supply store, or just use grocery bags) and mark it up with cave drawings of things like stick-figure people throwing spears at woolly mammoths (leave markers out so guests can make drawings of their own). Use remnants of fake fur, suede, and animal prints from the fabric store to drape over chairs and couches and throw on the floor as rugs. Light a fire in the fireplace if you have one. If not, place a bunch of brown pillar candles of varying heights on a table, and encircle them with rocks, to create the look of a campfire.

Serve

Offer foods like turkey drumsticks, chicken wings, ribs, grilled kebabs, nuts, and berries in rustic-looking baskets. Give your drinks glacial appeal by chilling them in dramatic fashion: Buy an ice luge mold online, fill it with water, and put it in the freezer at least 24 hours before the party. When you take it out, you'll have a block of ice with two winding channels carved into it;

pour beverages in at the top and they'll be chilled by the time they reach the cups (or mouths!) waiting at the bottom.

Wear

Tell everyone to come dressed in caveperson chic with torn scraps of fake fur and suede attached to their clothes, or slung over one shoulder and belted with a leather cord. Look up images from the movies above for inspiration (but, uh, not for an accurate history lesson!).

Rated BC

Get inspiration for your party from these prehistoric flicks.

One Million Years B.C. (1966) • *Caveman* (1981) • *The Clan of the Cave Bear* (1986) • *Encino Man* (1992) • *10,000 B.C.* (2008) • *Year One* (2009)

PHOTO STATION

Since they'll be dressed for it, set up an area for guests to produce their own take on the often-caricatured drawing depicting humans evolving from apes. Clear a stretch of wall and post a banner at least six feet high reading "Evolution of Man." At the far left side of the space, position a stuffed gorilla or monkey on the floor. Then get four or five guests at a time to pose in a line, each one slightly more erect than the next.

52 Ancient Greece Toga Party

Linens-as-clothing has become a favorite party theme ever since the Delta fraternity, in the 1978 cult classic *Animal House*, violated double-secret probation to host an epic toga party. But there's more to a great toga party than just dressing the part. Take the white robe and crown of ivy back to its roots by setting your party against the backdrop of Ancient Greece.

Prep

Cover tables and chairs with white sheets, big bunches of real or fake purple grapes, and garlands of fake ivy—spray-paint the ivy gold if you want. To go all out, make your place look like the Acropolis with large white columns; get a pair of faux ones from a party store or make them yourself out of large boxes. Search thrift stores or eBay for cheap figurines or busts that you can spray-paint white and set on the columns to look like old statues.

Serve

Put out a buffet of traditional Greek foods, like pasteli (sesame seed and honey candy), spanakopita (spinach and feta wrapped in phyllo pastry), and olives in olive oil for bread-dipping. Ancient Greek literature refers to "ambrosia" and "nectar" as the food and drink of the gods, so serve the modern versions: ambrosia salad and peach and apricot nectars.

Do

Strike up an appropriately godly game. Check out the rules for "Mr. Wizard" in the Meteor Shower Viewing Party on page 94; change the name to "Oracle" (as in the Greek's Oracle of Delphi) and you've got the perfect pastime to go with your ancient garb.

Wear

Tell people to come dressed for a trip to Mount Olympus—everyone should arrive in a toga-centric costume as a god or goddess, a character from Greek literature or legend, or a famous Greek philosopher or thinker. Here are some ideas.

A muse (goddess who inspires art, music, or literature). Toga plus any lyre- or flutelike instrument.

Atlas (titan who carried the world on his shoulders). Toga plus a large beach ball painted blue and green to look like a globe.

Achilles (hero of *The Iliad's* Trojan War). Toga plus a fake arrow affixed to the back of your ankle.

Artemis (goddess of the hunt). Toga plus toy bow and arrow.

Hippocrates (ancient Greek doctor known as the father of medicine). Toga plus a toy stethoscope.

53 Old Hollywood Party

Think of classic Hollywood, and a black-and-white image no doubt comes to mind. A few color films were made as early as the teens and 20s, but even after Dorothy walked out the door into rainbow-hued Munchkin Land in 1939, plenty of movies—and TV shows—were still filmed solely in shades of gray. Take your friends back to the Golden Age at a party where the room, the food, and even the guests themselves appear to be untouched by time or Technicolor.

Prep

Make guests feel like they're inside an old, precolor film or TV show by covering as many surfaces as possible in black, white, and gray. The easiest place to do this may be a sparsely decorated basement, where you can drape any walls and furniture with sheets. Then bring in props like a toy or homemade clapboard (that thing the guy slaps down as he says "take 37!"), film canisters, and vintage cameras, if you know anyone who collects them. Make your own version of the famous "Hollywood" sign to hang on your wall or front lawn.

Serve

Keep the look going with munchies like white and dark chocolate, black licorice, white powdered-sugar donut holes, New York City-style black-and-white cookies, and cola and clear lemon-lime soda in pitchers or a punch bowl.

Wear

Tell guests to come dressed as any character from a black-and-white movie like *Casablanca*, an old John Wayne western, a '50s sitcom like *I Love Lucy*, or a silent film from cinema's early days. The twist, though, is that they must wear *only* black, white, and gray, just as the characters appeared on film. For example, a Dorothy costume (from the *first* part of the *The Wizard of Oz*): Her blue-and-white checkered dress becomes a gray-and-white checkered dress, and the ruby slippers should be black.

Make Your Own Movies

Set up a video camera in a corner along with some silent movie props (a length of rope, a ladies' fan, a toy gun) and a sign explaining the instructions: One or two guests at a time should get in position, press Record, then ham it up like actors in a silent movie for 10 to 15 seconds. They should tell a mini-story, compensating for the lack of dialogue with exaggerated facial expressions and demonstrative movements. Play some old-timey piano music in the background and provide a small blackboard and white chalk so guests can create "intertitles"—funny dialogue they'll hold up to the camera before or after their scene. Post the finished "films" online.

54 '60s Woodstock Party

In the summer of 1969, hippie flower children from all across the country descended on a farm in Bethel, New York, for a momentous, outdoor, three-day music festival held in the name of peace, love, and rock 'n' roll. The festival was called Woodstock and it went down in history as one of the wildest, most legendary concerts of all time, drawing more than 30 musical acts and 400,000 people. The '60s might be over, but you can keep the memory of Woodstock alive by throwing your own version right at home.

Prep

Transform your living room into the back of a psychedelic Volkswagen van. Create this den of free love by laying out colorful tapestries and pillows on the floor and stringing love beads from the light fixtures. Replace the bulbs with black lights and hang black-light posters (designed to glow bright colors under the purple-ish lights) on the walls. Play a lava lamp DVD on your laptop or pick up a real one.

Wear

Tell your friends to come decked out in hippie fashions: low-rider bell-bottom jeans, tie-dye shirts, peasant blouses, and fringed vests. Wear your hair superlong and pin-straight or in a wild afro, and top it off with a ring of flowers or a bandana. Complete the look with a bunch of beaded necklaces and peace-sign accessories.

Serve

There was a major food shortage at the original Woodstock, so a peace activist known as Wavy Gravy stepped in to organize free brown rice, veggies, and granola. Be like Wavy, and serve these staples to your hungry masses.

Do

Rain turned Woodstock into a giant, mud-slicked playground. Create the same thing in your backyard by hosing down a nongrassy area with water. Or set up a long stretch of plastic tarp on the lawn, throw on some fake-mud powder, aim a hose at it, and let your friends slide down the muddy strip after a running start. In the background, play music from the bands that took the stage back in '69 by starting with the Peace and Love Playlist on this page. To complete the experience, camp out together in your living room—or right there in the backyard.

Peace and Love Playlist

"Star Spangled Banner" (Jimi Hendrix) • "With a Little Help From My Friends" (Joe Cocker) • "Evil Ways" (Santana) • "Piece of My Heart" (Janis Joplin) • "White Rabbit" (Jefferson Airplane) • "Suite: Judy Blue Eyes" (Crosby, Stills & Nash) • "The Weight" (The Band) • "Let's Work Together" (Canned Heat) • "Turn On Your Lovelight" (Grateful Dead) • "Bad Moon Rising" (Creedence Clearwater Revival) • "Everyday People" (Sly & the Family Stone) • "My Generation" (The Who)

55 '80s Teen Movie Party

The 1980s was the golden era of high school movies. It was all about the haves and the have-nots, the jocks and the geeks, the party kids who were hooking up and the shy ones who wanted to be. All of that along with sky-high mall hair, fingerless gloves, acid-washed jeans, and shoulder pads! Revisit the totally tubular teen flicks of the '80s with this old-school costume party.

Wear

Tell everyone to come as a character from an old-school teen movie. Try to match your costume to the scenes that make each character instantly recognizable (hint: props will be key). Here are a few ideas.

Say Anything... Go as Lloyd Dobler in a long trench coat holding a boombox over your head.

Ferris Bueller's Day Off. Be Sloane Peterson by wearing a cropped white jacket, white boots (bonus points if they have fringe), and Bermuda-length shorts.

Sixteen Candles. Wear a lavender dress and blonde wig with a chunk cut out of it to be Caroline, Jake Ryan's popular, drunk girlfriend who gets her hair stuck in a closed door at the big party.

PHOTO STATION

Designate an area for staging pictures of each set of characters posed as they are on the movie's video cover, or in a particular character's classic scene. Set up a photo op with a banner at just-overhead height that reads "Now on VHS!"

Risky Business. All you need to be Tom Cruise's character, Joel, is a pair of tube socks, a pink, striped button-down, a candlestick, and the guts to go out pants-less.

The Lost Boys. Wear a leather jacket, single dangly earring, and fangs to be one of the vampires; or just wear a camouflage shirt and red bandana around your forehead under your bangs—instant Corey Feldman.

Have even more fun with your costumes (and make them even more recognizable) by getting a group together to go as all the characters from one movie. For example, dress as the motley crew from *The Breakfast Club* or break out the shoulder-padded blazers and dress as the clique from *Heathers*.

Pump Up The Volume Playlist

Song	Movie
"Footloose"	*Footloose*
"Don't You (Forget About Me)"	*The Breakfast Club*
"In Your Eyes"	*Say Anything…*
"The Goonies 'R' Good Enough"	*The Goonies*
"If You Leave"	*Pretty in Pink*
"Old Time Rock 'N' Roll"	*Risky Business*
"The Power of Love"	*Back to the Future*
"Oh Yeah"	*Ferris Bueller's Day Off*
"Cry Little Sister"	*The Lost Boys*

56 Clothing Swap

Got a closet full of stuff you can't stand to look at anymore? Throw a swap party. This is a get-together where everyone brings their no-longer-wanted clothing items to trade. One friend's trash becomes another friend's treasure, and everyone goes home with new gear! Modern-day clothing swaps became popular when stylish city women who were overspending on clothes realized that swapping meant they could score shopping bags full of new outfits without spending a dime. How much loot will you leave the party with?

Prep

Tell your pals to bring over the clothes, jewelry, shoes, bags and other accessories that they never use anymore, but are still in good condition—nothing that is stained, smelly, ripped, or otherwise unwearable. In the room where you hold the party, be sure there's at least one full-length mirror available so everyone can see how they look in their potential swaps. (Bashful guests can change in the bathroom.)

Do

There are two ways to organize the swap. One is to lay out or hang up all the goods around the room so guests can "shop" boutique-style. The other is to have guests take turns presenting each of their items—preferably with not just size and brand info, but also with an entertaining story about why *they* can no longer use the item but why it would be fabulous on *you*. Other guests can raise their hands and snap up the item right away or wait till all the goods have been shown to pick and choose. At the end of the party, bag up the unclaimed clothes and donate them to a charity.

Serve

People get hungry when they shop, so serve up some munchies to keep everyone energized for the hunt. Look for cookie cutters shaped like dresses, hats, and high heels, or use a knife to cut T-shirt shapes out of sandwiches, forming mini crustless hors d'oeuvres. Another option: Buy little plastic dolls at a party supply store and stick them in cupcakes that have been frosted to look like skirts.

How to Deal With a "Bitch"

A clothing swap is sometimes called a "bitch" swap because when people fight it out over a popular item, it's called "bitching." Here's how to run the official "bitch" process: All interested parties try the piece on and the other guests (gently, despite the name) determine who wears it best, and she gets to keep it. Another way to settle the dispute is to simply allow the person who has accumulated fewer items at the swap to go home with the garment in question.

57 Just-the-Girls Spa Night

"Spa" is actually the name of a town in the Liège province of Belgium. People have been going there in droves to enjoy the great mineral springs ever since the 16th century, and over the years its name has become synonymous with any kind of health resort. Today, spas are big business, with some charging hundreds of dollars for a single treatment. But why pay a pro? You can have much more fun by hosting your own night of beautification right in your bedroom!

Prep

Hit the drugstore to pick up facial masks and body scrubs, or make them on your own. For a quick mask, try mixing up bananas, yogurt, and honey (the leftovers taste delicious!). For a DIY scrub, combine equal parts of any type of sugar or salt with an oil (baby, coconut, or vegetable oil work well). Since it's not sanitary to share certain beauty tools with other people, tell your friends to bring their own makeup, hair, and nail stuff.

Serve

Spas typically put out a pitcher of ice water with lemon slices for clients waiting for their services, as well as little healthy nibbles like nuts, dried fruit, and crackers. While you're at it, don't forget to slice a few cucumbers for your eyes!

Do

Spa treatments typically begin with steam to open the pores. Have everyone change into their bathing suits, then pile into the bathroom together, close the

door, and turn on the shower as hot as it'll go. In a minute or two, you'll have your own private steam bath. Use the body scrubs, rinse off, and get back into your dry robes before applying the facial masks. While you wait for them to soak in, retreat to another room, light some scented candles, lay back, place two cucumber slices on your eyelids, and bliss out to some tunes.

After your facial treatments are rinsed off, it's mani, pedi, and makeup time. Now's the perfect chance to experiment on one another with different colors and techniques, since you don't have to leave the house should your new look not turn out quite as expected. Of course, you'll most likely look fabulous, so finish the night with a photo shoot while everyone's all glammed up.

Girl-Bonding Playlist

For the exfoliation and makeup phase.

"Girls Just Want to Have Fun" (Cyndi Lauper) • "We Are Family" (Sister Sledge) • "Wannabe" (Spice Girls) • "You're My Best Friend" (Queen)

For the relaxation phase.

"Only Time" (Enya) • "Hide and Seek" (Imogen Heap) • "Sadeness, Pt. 1" (Enigma) • "Sweet Lullaby" (Deep Forest)

58 Extreme Room Makeover

Is your room still decorated with pink bows, superheroes, or choo-choo trains? If so, it may be time for a redo (provided that your parents are down with it!). But don't go it alone. Invite some friends over, serve up some food and music, and have everyone take part in your room re-creation. You get a killer party and a fresh, new space all at once!

Prep

First, measure your room to the nearest inch, as well as each major piece of furniture. Then, on a piece of paper, sketch out the walls of your space at a scale of 1:1—that is, for every foot of wall, draw an inch on the paper. Do the same, roughly, for the furniture on a separate piece of paper, and cut each piece out. Now you have a model with which you can decide how to rearrange the room and figure out the perfect setup before doing any heavy lifting.

Next, pick out and buy your new paint colors along with any painting supplies you don't have. Try to use a paint-and-primer-in-one product; otherwise, you'll have to wait a day or so in between putting up the primer coat and the actual color coat. Invite your friends over for a sleepover the night before the painting is to begin, and tell them to wear clothes they don't mind wrecking. Last, before everyone arrives, cover the furniture and floors in your room with sheets or drop-clothes and tape off window frames and other molding with painter's tape to protect everything from splatters.

Do

Half the fun of creating a new space is trashing the old one! So spend the night tagging your walls in graffiti and inventive art. Stick to pencils (or the new paint color) so you'll have no trouble painting over it. Take plenty of pictures before you crash, because by tomorrow afternoon, it'll all be gone. During the party, take out the room blueprint you made and get everyone's input on how to arrange your stuff for the coolest space. Then, after breakfast the next morning, crank up the music and start painting. As for rearranging your furniture into its new formation, you'll have to wait until all of the paint dries.

"Chi" Sheet

Feng shui is the ancient Chinese art of arranging your environment to harmonize with spiritual energy, known as chi. Want your bedroom makeover to really pay off? Here are a few ideas.

- To strengthen relationships: Place a pair of items (two figurines, vases, whatever) in the back right corner of your room.
- To improve your reputation: Place cone- or diamond-shaped objects in the center back area of your room (for example, a square pillow turned on its diagonal).
- To earn more money: Place a green plant in the back left corner of your room.

59 Mystery Tour

In their 1967 movie *Magical Mystery Tour*, The Beatles boarded a wacky, tricked-out bus for a very indirect journey to the beach. Let their long, strange trip be your inspiration for a mobile party and take your friends on the road for a day of surprise adventures. (P.S. You can do this by foot or public transportation as well, if you don't have a license yet or want to bring more than a carload of buddies.)

Prep

For this party, you'll be planning a day's worth of events, but only you (and a coconspirator, if you choose one) will know the itinerary. So when you invite your friends, tell them only what time to be ready, what time they'll be home, and what to bring (like a bathing suit, if you're going swimming, or some cash if you're going somewhere that requires entrance fees or purchasing food).

Do

Visit the tourism website for your city or state to dig up local hidden gems you never knew existed (try RoadsideAmerica.com as well for "oddball attractions"). Aim for at least three different stops. Here are a few ideas.

- an out-of-the-way swimming hole or a fancy hotel for pool hopping
- a roller-skating rink or duckpin bowling alley
- anything that requires getting on a ferry, whether auto or pedestrian

- a trailhead to a scenic outlook
- a quirky museum, like the Burlingame Museum of Pez Memorabilia in California or Leila's Hair Museum in Independence, Missouri
- an airbrush tattoo stand
- a pottery-painting place

Once you've got a game plan, print out directions or plug addresses into a GPS and begin your journey!

Road Trip Playlist

"Magical Mystery Tour" (The Beatles) • "Roam" (The B-52's) • "Truckin'" (Grateful Dead) • "Slow Ride" (Foghat) • "Route 66 (Beatmasters Mix)" (Depeche Mode) • "On the Road Again" (Willie Nelson) • "Drive My Car" (The Beatles) • "Where the Streets Have No Name" (U2)

Road Games

During long stretches in between destinations, play road trip games. Try 1/100, where you count how many people you'd be willing to date out of the next 100 guys or girls you pass. Or play classic Punch Buggy, in which you get to chuck a fellow passenger on the shoulder when you spot a Volkswagen Beetle before they do; if a backseat rider racks up 5 punches, they get to take over shotgun.

60 Vegas-Inspired Night

S*wingers. Ocean's Eleven. The Hangover.* Why do so many cinematic adventures take place in Las Vegas? Maybe it's because the possibility of winning big makes everything just a little more thrilling. So shuffle your deck, practice your dealer lingo, and bring the fun home by hosting your own kitchen-table poker tournament. Vegas, baby!

Prep

Create a poker table by buying a few yards of green felt at the fabric store, stretching it tightly over your dining room table, and duct-taping it to the underside. You'll also need a deck of cards (obviously) and chips to bet with. (You could also play with spare change that would stand in for various denominations of poker chips.)

Full House Playlist

"Poker Face" (Lady Gaga) • "The Gambler" (Kenny Rogers) • "That Was a Crazy Game of Poker" (O.A.R.) • "Leaving Los Vegas" (Sheryl Crow) • "House of the Rising Sun" (The Animals) • "Two of Hearts" (Stacey Q) • "Black Jack Davey" (The White Stripes) • "Wakin' Up in Vegas" (Katy Perry)

If you and all your friends are new to card playing, familiarize yourselves with a few variations of the game before the party, like Texas hold'em, five-card draw, or seven-card stud. Look up the rules and make sure you know the basics by heart so that play runs smoothly; to help your guests, print out a cheat sheet showing the rank-order of hands (pairs, straights, flushes, etc.) and put it in a frame on the table where everyone can see it.

Do

Once everyone's at the table, order a pizza, put out some chips, and explain the rules to those who haven't played before. While some poker clubs have members buy into the game with a set sum of cash, like $20, simply betting with chips not tied to any real money may be easier for beginners (not to mention more legal if you're all minors). Start out by giving everyone the same number of chips, then play round after round until all but one player has gone bust.

Poker Terms to Know

- **Ante.** The money every player is required to bet at the beginning of each round.
- **Raise.** To bet more money than the minimum required, forcing every other player to do the same if they want to stay in the game.
- **Call.** To bet only as much money as the players before you to stay in the game.
- **Fold.** To quit the round by placing your cards face down on the table, rather than bet more money and risk losing.
- **Bluff.** To fool your opponents into either betting more or folding.

61 Obscure Holiday Party

Sure, parties for Christmas, New Year's, and Halloween are great, but it takes a true original to throw a National Cream-Filled Donut Day party (that's on September 14, by the way) or a fete in honor of Extraterrestrial Culture Day (the second Tuesday in February, per order of the New Mexico House of Representatives). So why wait for a mainstream occasion? Find a more obscure reason for celebration, and go all out with it!

Prep

Choose a random holiday (there are lots of lists online). You could go with a less-observed yet legit one, like Flag Day on June 14, which could be a fun excuse to celebrate with your friends if you're all going separate ways for July 4th. Or go with a wackier, only semiofficial one. Here are a few ideas to get you thinking.

Hug a GI Day, March 4. Get it? March *forth*? If you live near a military base or training center, gather some friends and some homemade cookies and station yourselves near the entrance. Otherwise, host an all-camo costume party and hug it out there.

Van Gogh's Birthday, March 30. Have your friends over for a painting party—no ear-sacrifice required.

Birthday of Marshmallow Fluff, May 14. Make your own Fluffernutter sandwiches.

Blue Jeans' Birthday, May 20. Wear head-to-toe denim at a party honoring the day Levi Strauss got his jeans patent in 1873.

Christmas in June, June 25. Only six months till Santa comes—but who wants to wait? Throw a Christmas-themed party in the summer.

Dictionary Day, October 16. Have everyone come dressed in a costume representing a totally obscure SAT word—like a magician's outfit for "prestidigitation" (that's sleight of hand) or a ton of jangly bracelets and anklets for "tintinnabulation" (that's the ringing of bells).

Party for a Cause

Awareness days and months are worth celebrating, too. Here are three to think about.

Breast Cancer Awareness Month, anytime in October. Have a pink party, where everyone wears the signature color, to raise money for a breast cancer charity like the Susan G. Komen for the Cure foundation.

Earth Day, April 22. Make your event green in every way: Require guests to come in outfits completely made up of recycled items like thrift-shop clothes, used printer paper, or (clean!) cloth baby diapers.

National Volunteer Blood Donor Month, anytime in January. Organize an outing to a blood drive for your 17-and-older friends (16 with parental permission in some states), then have everyone back to your place for cookies and hot cocoa to rehydrate and recuperate. Or throw the Blood Bash on page 36 and give everyone who shows up with an "I donated blood today" sticker an extra goodie bag.

62 Initiation Party

Whether you're on a sports team, in the marching band, on an academic team, or in a performance group, suffering through the tryouts for potential new members can be torturous and exhausting: staying long hours after school, meeting hordes of incoming freshman, and bearing the stress of having to reject people who don't make the cut. But once tryouts (and hell week!) are finally over, it's time to forget all that, bond as a group, and officially usher in the new team members! Welcome the newbies in style by throwing them an initiation party they won't forget.

Prep

Your initiation event should have all the elements of any great get-together—music, munchies, and hanging out together as a team. Beforehand, make each veteran player a secret mentor to a younger player. In the days leading up to the party, the mentor secretly decorates the newbie's locker and/or leaves little presents or messages of encouragement in his or her backpack or gear bag. At the party, the mentors reveal their identities to the newbies (see Do).

If you want to make it a surprise party, coordinate with the freshmen's parents to "kidnap" them at an unexpected time. After you've picked up all of the new team members, head over to the party together.

Do

Apart from simply celebrating and getting to know the new people, you can also take part in these initiation rites.

Nicknames. Hold a ceremony at the party where the upperclassmen bestow an official team nickname on each new player, based on their personality or inside jokes and funny stuff that's happened during training so far.

Talent Show. Have the new kids put on a skit or funny song routine for the upperclassmen (or vice versa!).

Mentor Revelation. Have a ceremony in which the newly chosen mentors (see Prep) reveal their identities.

A Bit Haze-y

Upperclassmen sometimes put new team members through certain initiation rites, but it's important that you don't cross the line over into hazing. Don't do anything that can cause humiliation, fear, or pain to an incoming team member. Even stuff that you might do with friends for fun (making someone swallow the contents of 10 ketchup packets or "moon" someone else out of a car window) can really screw up a teammate if they feel forced to do it. It can also hurt team morale and get you in trouble with the school or law. In planning your party, be extra careful that everything you do is clearly designed to make new members feel welcomed with open arms.

63 Pre-Game Carbo-Loading Party

Carbo-loading is sort of an old-school notion. The theory was that a heaping plate of carbs, like pasta, the day before a big athletic event would provide muscles with extra fuel. But most trainers now believe you can get the same or higher energy levels just by eating a well-balanced diet. Still, it's fun to get psyched up for a big game by socializing (and chowing down!) with your teammates. Whether you're on a sports team, or prepping for an academic event, host a team-building pre-game party.

Prep

Two nights before you're scheduled to take down your cross-town rival, invite everyone over to your place to rally. If cooking for the entire team stresses you out, consider making it a potluck where everyone brings one piece of the meal: Assign beverages to the freshmen, appetizers to the sophomores, side dishes to the juniors, and main dishes to the seniors. Before everyone arrives, set up a buffet in your kitchen or dining room with plates, glasses, utensils, and napkins.

Serve

One easy, well-balanced dish to feed a crowd is pasta with marinara sauce and cooked vegetables. Don't forget a salad and some nice crusty bread, as well.

If you want to step it up a notch, look online to find a place that has pasta in the shape of an item from your sport or activity, like soccer balls, baseball gloves, football helmets, or trumpets.

Do

If you're not on a team with a dedicated cheer squad (or if your team *is* the cheer squad!), make your own banners advertising the big game. After dinner, set out a big bunch of paints, markers, and alphabet stencils, along with poster boards to create signs for the school hallways and/or fans in the bleachers. You may need permission to hang things on the walls, so check in with the school administration before putting anything up.

Get Pumped Playlist

"Eye of the Tiger" (Survivor) • "Gonna Fly Now (Theme from Rocky)" (Bill Conti) • "We Will Rock You" (Queen) • "Lose Yourself" (Eminem) • "Tubthumping" (Chumbawamba) • "Blitzkrieg Bop" (Ramones) • "The Distance" (Cake) • "Song 2" (Blur) • "Don't Stop Believin'" (Journey)

64 Ultimate Tailgate Party

You don't need a house to throw a great party—you can throw one out of the back of your car. That's known as a tailgate party, and it's become such a part of the stadium experience that it can supersede the game itself as the main event. So do it up right, show your team pride, and make your car *the* place to be.

Prep

First, look up the stadium's tailgating rules. These will tell you where you're allowed to have a tailgate party and when you can arrive. Get there right at opening so you'll have your pick of spots. Look for one that gives you a little extra room, like on the end of a row, and one near (but not too near!) the bathrooms.

Great tailgates run the gamut from totally low-tech to fully equipped rides with everything from built-in grills to portable generators powering flat-screen TVs so you can play *Madden* before going in to watch the real thing. But only a few things are absolutely essential for a good time. First off, seating. Lawn chairs work, but if you have a truck, you can also pile up the back of the bed with old couch cushions. (Or, hey, load the whole

Rock On

Parking lot partying isn't just for sports: Some of the most extreme tailgates are said to take place outside Jimmy Buffett concerts, where fans bring in sand, palm trees, and hammocks to match the beachy theme of their favorite singer's music!

couch in there!) If your vehicle's not a hatchback or truck, you'll need a folding table in addition to seating. You'll also need a way to play music, like a speaker dock for your MP3 player.

Pimp Your Ride

Since your vehicle is the center of the party, make sure to deck it out in team-spirited paraphernalia. Tag it with window-glass markers or stick-on decals in your team's colors and look online to find removable car stickers (that can be customized for your school), neoprene ice chest covers, and other fun stuff that will draw attention to your car.

Serve

If all you've got is a Styrofoam cooler, snacks like subs, chips, and dips always work. Got a crock pot? Cook up some chili. A portable grill is great for burgers and kabobs. But for extra parking lot props, create your own original, over-the-top dish. For example, expand a favorite recipe with a twist; if 7-layer dip (refried beans, shredded cheese, tomatoes, avocado, black olives, green onions, and sour cream) is good, wouldn't 16-layer dip be even better?

Do

Aside from eating, lawn games like cornhole, washers, and ladder golf are the backbone of every awesome tailgate (ironic, since they're usually held on asphalt!). Also check out The Perfect Picnic on page 104 for more game ideas.

65 Powder Puff Party

The Powder Puff game is an annual tradition at many schools in which senior girls face off against the junior girls in a touch football match while the male players dress up and stand in as cheerleaders. Powder Puff events are sometimes held as after-school fundraisers, but yours could just be an awesome, cross-dressing pep-rally party to get everyone—athletes or not—pumped up a couple days before the biggest game of the season.

Prep

Decorate your place (or a nearby park if you don't have a yard big enough for a football game) with school colors, pendants, and banners. Create a mini playing field, with end zones marked by cones or anything bright and unbreakable. If you want a full cheering section, invite not just team members but all your friends, whether they're into playing or just being spectators.

Wear

Girls wear football-appropriate athletic wear like sneakers, capri stretch pants, and a jersey (with a set of shoulder pads underneath, if they can score a pair). Supply a tube of eye-black—or black lipstick!—for them to smudge on below their bottom lashes for authenticity. The guys should come in cheer garb. Talk to the cheerleading coach about any spare large-size uniforms left in

the equipment closet, or hit up the nearest Goodwill (skirts don't have to zip up all the way—a couple big safety pins can bridge the gap).

Serve

Fill little paper cups with beverages out of a cooler jug, sidelines-style. For football-themed snack ideas, see Super Bowl Party, page 146.

Do

Play! For the girls, it's a knock-down, drag-out grudge match (without any actual knocking down or dragging—it's just touch football!). For the guys, it's a chance to show off their attempts at jumps and splits, creatively rhymed cheers, and a likely top-heavy human pyramid. Put out blank poster boards and markers for them to make what are sure to be interesting cheer signs as well. The game doesn't have to take all night—set an alarm clock or kitchen timer for two 15-minute halves.

The Miss Heisman

If you want to make your Powder Puff party an annual event, build a funny trophy that can be passed from one winning team to the next—like a makeup compact (you know, the kind that holds a powder puff) glued open and then super-glued to the base of an old elementary school trophy you don't care about anymore. Spray-paint the compact metallic gold to look like the real thing.

66 Move-It-or-Lose-It Party

Wii Sports parties are common these days. But do you ever stop and think, as you're swinging your racquetless hand through the air to get a virtual ball over a net made purely of colored pixels—*Hey, we could be playing actual tennis right now instead?* On your next birthday or a random weekend, press Pause and throw a party that will get everyone's heart pumping. Life is not a spectator sport!

Do

Active party options abound! Here are a few to consider.

Bowling. With food and an arcade, bowling alleys are a great bet—especially ones that offer late-night, weekend disco bowling, where the lights are dimmed and the music cranked up. If you're a new bowler, investigate alleys that have duckpin bowling, which uses little balls and pins.

Yoga. Hire an instructor to give you and your friends a private lesson at your place or in the studio. Ask everyone to chip in for the fee. If you can hold it on someone's deck at sunset or in the early morning after a sleepover, even better!

Ice Skating. You don't have to wait till winter—indoor rinks often offer discounts during summer. Just don't head out onto any old frozen pond unless you're sure the ice is super solid.

Wear

Make sure everyone knows to come dressed and prepped to play—socks for bowling, mat for yoga, hat and gloves for skating. Have guests bring a change of clothes, too, if you want to hang out after.

Serve

For a warm-weather party, grill outdoors afterward, or pack a picnic lunch. Following a yoga party (indoors or out), think healthy, plant-based, organic munchies, like cucumber and avocado sandwiches and fresh fruit salad. For an outdoor, wintertime party, serve treats afterward to warm everyone back up—a steaming pot of hot cocoa with all the fixings (to create a cocoa bar, see Winter Wonderland on page 44) or a bubbling crock of cheese or chocolate fondue (see page 108). Soup or chili are great ideas if your party runs through a mealtime since they're warm, hearty, and easy to make in large batches.

Fun Run

Bored with your usual run? Invite your friends and make it a "hash" instead. Hash House Harriers are irreverent running clubs where members ("hounds") follow a winding—and sometimes misleading and thorny—trail of flour laid by the "hare" to a secret party spot where snacks and beverages await. Why not lead your fellow cross-country friends on an off-season mystery run with a party of your own at the end?

67 Super Bowl Party

The very first Super Bowl game was played in Los Angeles on January 15, 1967, between the Kansas City Chiefs and the victorious Green Bay Packers. But there were no big-name halftime acts (and probably no wardrobe malfunctions either!). More than four decades later, the celebrities, commercials, and munchies are as much a part of Super Bowl Sunday fun as the game itself. Your party will combine all elements to make it a top-notch football-fest.

Prep

Heighten the good-natured rivalry between teams by drawing a line down the center of the room with masking tape, a la bickering siblings. Put one team's cheer section on the left and the other on the right; no food, drink, or people may pass over the line, unless they agree to officially convert! (Gotta pee? Better hop over the back of the sofa unless you want to be labeled a traitor.) Do up the rest of the room in each side's team colors. Or, use their mascots as a theme instead: an ocean motif for the Miami Dolphins, pirate stuff for the Tampa Bay Buccaneers, angel wings and halos for the New Orleans Saints, etc. Give out swag, like team-color Mardi Gras beads, foam fingers, glow sticks, and noisemakers.

Serve

Serve anything from really great-tasting game food (like wings, potato skins, chips, and dips) to football-themed cupcakes. Or provide regional dishes from each team's city—like a bubbling pot of New England clam chowder for the Patriots, cheesesteaks for the Philadelphia Eagles, or deep dish pizza for the Chicago Bears. Wash it all down with bottles of Gatorade, a sideline fixture.

A Word From Our Sponsors

More into the big-budget commercials than the game? Make a set of rating cards (1–5) for each guest, and ask everyone to rate the ads as they appear. Keep track and see which ones got the highest score at the end.

Do

For traditional Super Bowl betting ("the pool"), draw up a grid with 100 boxes; let people buy boxes in the grid for a quarter apiece by writing their initials inside them. Once they're all filled in, label the top row with the numbers zero through nine in random order (representing the last digit of the score of the American Football Conference team), and do the same down the left-hand side (representing the last digit of the score of the National Football Conference team). If the score is 31 to 17, for example, and your initials are in the box where the 1 row and the 7 column meet, you win the pot! Select a winner for the score at the end of each quarter and, at the end of the game, split up the pot accordingly.

68 Oscar Night Soiree

From the red carpet fashion analysis to the celeb-filled after-parties, the Oscars are the granddaddy of all awards ceremonies—every movie actor's dream and movie lover's event of the year. Throw your own Academy Awards bash with these ideas and you'll need a prepared acceptance speech to thank everyone for all the compliments.

Prep

For a real star-studded affair, glitz up the place with anything gold and/or sequined; steal prop ideas from the Old Hollywood Party, page 118, or the event-arrival photo station from the Ultimate Cast Party, page 164.

Serve

For food, channel past episodes of TBS's *Dinner and a Movie* to come up with clever names for snacks or drinks pegged to each Best Picture nominee, like Nacho Planet for the science fiction epic, *Avatar,* or Hotdogs Zillionaire for the rags-to-riches story, *Slumdog Millionaire*.

Do

Here are three showtime activities.

Rate the Stars. Write the numbers 1–10 on pieces of construction paper; make a full set for each guest. Then use them as scorecards to rate the stars' outfits during the red carpet arrivals show before the ceremony.

Winner Prediction. Download the current year's ballot from Oscars.org and make a copy for each of your guests to fill out, so you can see who makes the most correct predictions.

Kiss, Marry, or Kill. When the nominees are shown for each category, you must choose one person you'd kiss, one person you'd marry, and one person you'd kill (not for real, obviously!). Let everyone shout out their answers or go around the room taking turns with each award category.

Make a game out of spotting Oscar clichés, too. For example: You probably don't have enough couch seating around the TV for everyone and will have to resort to camp chairs, bean bags, and floor space; so make a rule that anytime a winner either cries during their acceptance speech or tries to talk over the wrap-it-up music, everyone has to get up and scramble for a new seat.

An Honor Just Being Nominated

One of the perks for nominees attending the Oscars is the lavish gift basket each one gets—valued in the $100,000 range—stocked full of freebies from companies hoping the recipients will promote their products. Create your own swag bag by asking each guest to bring one cool, not-too-expensive item to add; it could be a mix CD, funky sunglasses, or your famous brownies. Award the loot to the person who wins the Oscar ballot contest.

69 Season Premiere/Finale Viewing Party

You and your friends have been loyal viewers of your favorite show all season long—maybe even for years—and now it's all coming to a big, epic climax. Either that, or you've been missing your beloved characters for months in the off-season, patiently waiting for their return in the fall or spring premiere. Instead of each of you just parking it on the couch and watching all alone, get together for a fan-tastic viewing party.

Prep

Figure out who among you has the best home-theater environment and set up camp there—it could be the person with the big-screen TV or the basement free of parents and siblings constantly needing to be caught up on the characters and plot. (Speaking of: Set a rule for first-time-viewer friends that questions are allowed only during commercials!)

Serve

Have fun with thematic TV snacks. If it's a crime drama, use a huge water gun as a soda fountain to pour drinks into cups. For a musical show like *Glee*, find chocolate molded into microphone shapes or arrange white and milk chocolate bar segments into a mini piano keyboard on the coffee table. Party and toy stores are great places to look for novelty sweets to fit specific themes, like cell phone gum dispensers and candy lipsticks for a *Gossip Girl* party.

Do

To make viewing even more fun, play a game pegged to the quirks of your series. Create a slightly different bingo card for each of your friends; instead of numbers, fill the squares with classic catchphrases or events that may (or usually do) happen on your show. Like for *Mad Men*, spaces could say things like "Betty and Don fight" or "A secretary cries." Everyone checks off their card as they watch until someone gets five squares in a row—bingo!

Marathon

In the middle of a TV season? Hold a complete-series marathon instead, where you watch all the episodes of an old series (or as many as you can squeeze into one night) on DVD back to back! One-season cult favorites about high school, like *Freaks and Geeks* or *My So-Called Life*, work particularly well.

70 Karaoke Party

You've been caught belting out your favorite song on the radio when stopped at the traffic light. You rock a shampoo-bottle mic in the shower like nobody's business. It's time to share that talent with the rest of the world—or at least six to ten of your closest friends. If those *American Idol* first-rounders have the confidence to put it all out there, so can you!

Prep

Decide how you want to pipe in the music and lyrics for your karaoke party. Here are a few options:

Karaoke Machine. These play popular music without the vocals, while scrolling the lyrics of the songs on their own screen or on your TV. They usually come with a microphone, so you can sing along with some volume. Some DVD players even have a karaoke machine included.

Online Sites. These provide lyrics and music and let you record and share your performances with friends. You can also get microphones that connect to your computer speakers. If you can connect your computer to your TV, have the lyrics appear on the bigger TV screen, which is perfect for a party.

TV Access. If you have the Karaoke Channel's video on-demand service (which is available through many cable providers), you get instant karaoke right on your television—no laptop necessary!

Standing Ovation

Create an authentic concert experience: Give out lighters for people to spark up during ballads, and sling flowers and undies at your friends after they finish to make them laugh or do an encore.

PlayStation, Wii, Xbox, GameCube. Video games like SingStar and Karaoke Revolution come bundled with compatible microphones and let singers compete by judging how well they hit the notes, as well as record and share their performances. Some games also include the option to play fake instruments, which is great for people who don't love to sing.

Wear

Stock a table by the mic with rock-appropriate props like sunglasses, bandanas, and feather boas for people to incorporate into their acts. Or, consider giving your party a theme, like '80s hair bands or Woodstock, and have people dress the part.

Do

Designate an MC (short for "Master of Ceremonies") who takes requests, cues up numbers, and introduces performers. Make sure everyone's aware of proper karaoke etiquette: Don't hog the mic, duplicate a song that's already been sung, or—worst of all—criticize someone's singing. In fact, the off-key, silly, but spirited performances are the best ones of all.

71 Rocky Horror Picture Show Party

The Rocky Horror Picture Show is a raunchy rock musical about a naive newlywed couple (Brad and Janet) who get stranded at a house of singing and dancing eccentrics. It was considered a failure when it came out in 1975, but die-hard fans of the movie started congregating (in costume!) at the Waverly Theater in New York City's Greenwich Village to perform the movie at the screenings. This started a trend, and fans today still come dressed in full costume to act out the movie and perform elaborate audience-participation rituals at midnight showings. Keep the tradition alive by throwing your own Rocky Horror night!

Prep

If you've never seen *RHPS* in a theater, do that first to prepare yourself for your party. That night, you'll be known as a "virgin." At the start of the movie, all virgins are called up to be ritually initiated into the community (actors will do something silly like draw a "V" on your forehead or make you eat a Twinkie!). You'll also learn all the audience participation rituals. (If you can't go to a screening, rent the movie instead, check out rockyhorror.com, and see the prop list in Do).

Wear

People should come in costume as one of the characters, unless they're "virgins." If you're bold, go for Magenta in a French maid outfit and bushy wig, or Rocky in nothing but gold shorts. A little more timid? Do Brad or Janet in thick black glasses or a pretty pink dress, respectively.

Do

Hold your own initiation rites for the *Rocky* virgins, and then start the movie. Here's a cheat sheet to common *RHPS* props, and what scene to use them in the movie.

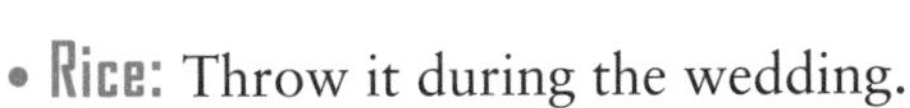

- **Rice:** Throw it during the wedding.
- **Newspaper:** Hold it over your head during the rainstorm.
- **Water guns:** Shoot them during the same scene to simulate rain.
- **Lighters:** Fire them up at the words "there's a light" in the song "Over at the Frankenstein Place."
- **Rubber gloves:** Snap them like Frank during the creation speech.
- **Noisemakers:** Blow them at the end of the same speech.
- **Confetti:** Toss it when the characters do at the end of the "Charles Atlas Song."
- **Toilet paper:** Send it flying when Dr. Scott enters the lab and Brad yells, "Great Scott!"
- **Toasted bread slices:** Hurl them when Frank proposes a toast.
- **Party hats:** Put 'em on when the characters do at the dinner table.
- **Deck of cards:** Scatter them at the words "cards for sorrow, cards for pain" in the song "I'm Going Home."

72 Film Festival

Watching one movie at home is a night in. Watch three or more—surrounded by all your friends piled on the couch together in front of the blue flickering screen—and it becomes a party. Take a cue from Sundance and hold a film festival one night in the dead of winter, when all you want to do is hole up inside, pop a little popcorn, and take part in some superior, social vegging.

Prep

Pick a theme, and then pick your flicks based on that. Some ideas for themes are: best new releases (like the Cannes International Film Festival in France), independent movies (like the Sundance Film Festival in Park City, Utah), foreign films (like the San Francisco International Film Festival), or documentaries (like the Hot Docs festival in Toronto, Canada). Feeling a little sillier? Do a Bad Movie Night full of guilty pleasures that are fun to hate, like *Snakes on a Plane* and *Showgirls*. Other ideas: your favorite heartthrob's early B-list movies, an evening of teen flicks from different decades, or parts one through three of your favorite adventure series. Either supply all the DVDs yourself, or have each of your friends bring one selection that fits the bill. Choose between two and four movies for the evening.

Serve

Make the snacks more interesting than your typical movie-night fare with a popcorn buffet: Pop up a big batch using an air popper (or use plain microwave popcorn), then offer toppings like regular salt, melted butter, garlic salt, powdered cheddar or parmesan, and sugar for kettle corn. For caramel corn, bring to a boil 1 cup brown sugar, ½ cup corn syrup, ½ cup butter, and ½ teaspoon salt, stirring the mix constantly. Let it boil without stirring for 5 minutes and then remove it from heat. Add a dash of vanilla extract and ½ teaspoon baking soda and stir; pour over popped popcorn. After the second movie, set up a coffee bar to help everyone stay awake for round three. Put out a pot of hot joe plus flavored creamers, sugar, whipped cream, cinnamon, caramel and chocolate syrup.

And the winner is...

Festivals aren't just about watching great movies; most are also a competition in categories like screenwriting and cinematography. At the end of the evening, choose a winner based on traditional categories, or give each movie its own unique prize, like Best Dialogue or Most Laughable Hairdos.

Do

In between screenings, make sure you take breaks to stretch your legs and talk about what you just watched. The cool thing about film festivals is that after seeing a bunch of movies all in one category, you can compare apples to apples. Are teen comedies getting racier or tamer as time goes on? Are sequels better than originals, or is the first always the best? Discuss!

73 Character Soundtrack Party

Wouldn't it be awesome if you went to a costume party dressed as Daisy Duke from *The Dukes of Hazzard* and "Dazzey Duks" by Duice just happened to come on? Who says you can't orchestrate those moments ahead of time? Create a built-in way to get people on the dance floor by throwing a TV/movie character-themed party and playing each guest's theme song at least once during the night.

Prep

On your invites, explain the premise of the party and ask everyone to tell you who they plan to dress as at least three or four days before the party, along with what song or songs they want you to add to the playlist for their character. Make sure that they only tell *you* who they'll be—it's more fun if they reveal their costumes to everyone else at the actual party.

Total Request Live

You can also do this party with just music and no costumes. Ask everyone to RSVP to your online invitation with their favorite movie theme song. Play them all at least once that night. Encourage people to come up with funny, random, and nostalgic selections (think *The Simpsons*, Disney movies, GEICO commercials), and you can be sure everyone will be singing and acting along.

Wear

Remind people that anything goes: They can use characters from cartoons, commercials, sitcoms, dramas, and films. If anyone needs inspiration, here are some ideas.

Be	Wear	Play
Alex from *Flash-dance*	Wet-look hair, '80s-dance-wear, bare feet	"Maniac" (Michael Sembello)
The title character from *Napoleon Dynamite*	Blonde curly wig, "Vote for Pedro" T-shirt	"Canned Heat" (Jamiroquai)
Penny Lane from *Almost Famous*	Fur coat, hippie love beads, round-framed "John Lennon" glasses	"Tiny Dancer" (Elton John)
The title character from *Juno*	Orange, striped T-shirt with fake pregnant belly (use a beach ball)	"All I Want Is You" (Barry Louis Polisar)

Also, not everyone has to be a specific character—for example, someone could come in scrubs and a toy stethoscope and request "How to Save a Life" by The Fray, associated with *Grey's Anatomy*.

74 Clip Show Party

A nightspot by the name of McCarthy's in Boston used to be known for this unique form of entertainment: Throughout the night, between song sets, they'd grab everyone's attention by killing the music and playing a great movie clip on the TV, then following it with an ingeniously matched song. It takes skills to pull this off—part TV producing, part DJing, and part party hosting—but it's a lot of fun making the whole thing work.

Prep

Use film clips that are about three minutes long, and are dramatic and compelling but without much soundtrack of their own. Start and end each clip at natural points so that someone who hasn't seen the movie or show can still get the gist of what's going on. You don't need to be editing-software savvy; often the exact clip you're looking for can be found on YouTube.

As for the corresponding song, it should be a fun and familiar one. Rather than always matching it perfectly to the mood or action in the segment, make some of your tunes serve as funny or irreverent reactions to the clip. The punchline can come right at the beginning of the song, or later in the chorus—leading to a one- or two-second delay as people then realize the brilliance of your choice.

Do

At the party, play music at a regular volume throughout the night. Every 20 minutes or so, cut it off so that everyone's focus is suddenly captured. Play your movie clip on the TV, followed immediately by the matching song. Make each clip-related song the first in a 20-minute playlist, so that the tunes flow seamlessly afterward; you'll know when it's time to get set for another clip when you hear the last song in the mix. Here are some movie/music matchup ideas to get you started.

Movie	Scene	Song
Stand by Me	The boys emerge from a pond covered in leeches—*everywhere*.	"Great Balls of Fire" (Jerry Lee Lewis)
Superbad	Tucked into sleeping bags, best friends Seth and Evan share how much they love each other Then, Seth "boops" Evan on the nose.	"I Got You Babe" (Sonny & Cher)
The Sixth Sense	At the little girl's funeral reception, her ghost directs Cole to play a video, which reveals that her mother had poisoned her.	"Bad Medicine" (Bon Jovi)
Kill Bill: Vol 1	Brought to her knees in a swordfight with O-Ren, The Bride gets a second wind, ultimately lopping off a slice of her opponent's skull.	"Hole in My Head" (Dixie Chicks)
Titanic	Rose realizes Jack's dead, lets him go into the icy water, and swims out toward the rescue boat.	"I'm on A Boat (featuring T-Pain)" (The Lonely Island)

75 Graffiti Party

While people have been scrawling on walls since caveman times, modern graffiti art got its start in Philly and New York in the 1960s and '70s, when artists tried to plaster their nicknames on as many subway cars as possible without getting hauled off by the cops. By the '80s, their inventive vandalism had started to become high art, eventually showing up in exhibits at places like the Museum of Modern Art. At this 21st-century graffiti party, you won't be tagging trains—you'll be tagging the blank canvases of your friends' T-shirts. Flesh and bones present different challenges than concrete and steel, but all the same illicit fun.

Prep

Pick an empty place, like an unfinished basement, and think gritty, urban retro for décor. Put out an old boombox (even if you play your '80s rap and hip-hop playlist on your laptop). Place flattened cardboard boxes on the ground to make a "dance floor" like in old break-dancing videos. Spray-paint the name of the party on a white sheet and hang it up, leaving plenty of blank space for artwork in the margins. Replace the regular bulbs in all your lamps with black light bulbs. The dim, purplish light they give off will make anything white or fluorescent (like highlighter ink) glow in the dark.

Tell each person to bring a permanent marker or highlighter, or just buy a few 10-packs yourself at an office supply store and scatter them around the party room for people to use. Neon (washable!) body paint can be fun, too; see what your local craft store has to offer.

Wear

On the invitation, tell the guests to wear white or mostly white shirts they don't care about wrecking. Men's undershirts work well, and you can find cheap multipacks to split with a few friends at any drugstore.

Do

Turn up the music and draw! Sign your name down someone's sleeve, draw a naughty cartoon around your best friend's navel, or write an anonymous love note across your crush's back where he or she can't see it till later. At the end of the night, you'll all have one-of-a-kind souvenirs signed by all of your friends. Of course, whether you're actually able to wear them out in public again depends on your friends' level of, um, "creativity."

Graffiti Party Playlist

"The Breaks" (Kurtis Blow) • "Rapper's Delight" • (The Sugarhill Gang) • "Mary, Mary" (Run-DMC) • "Push It" (Salt-N-Pepa) • "Fight for Your Right" (Beastie Boys) • "Parents Just Don't Understand" (DJ Jazzy Jeff & The Fresh Prince) • "Wild Thing" (Tone Loc) • "Bust a Move" (Young MC)

76 Ultimate Cast Party

The last night of a show is a natural high: You rocked the house, the pressure of the run is instantly gone, and all that's left to do is have fun. So where's the party? Every cast of every play should have a killer send-off!

Prep

The easiest place to throw a cast party is in a room off backstage, if one's available. If not, your place or a restaurant works, too. To decorate, hang rehearsal and performance photos on the walls, and add funny captions, arrows, and quotes.

Plan a mock awards ceremony for the party. To do this, work with another cast member to come up with a funny award for each person involved in the production, like Best Fake Crying, Best Supporting Undergarment, and Best Revival of a Play (given to your director, for reviving the production from the nearly comatose state it was in a week before opening).

Serve

People probably haven't eaten since late afternoon, and stress takes a lot out of you. Pick up the usual munchies, tell everyone they're welcome to bring a treat to share, and around lunchtime that day, call a pizza place to schedule a mega delivery for later that night.

Do

About a half hour into the party, ask the director to make a toast. Then, give anyone who wants it a chance to thank others who made the show a success. After the more sincere thank-yous are over, announce the mock awards and allow each recipient to make an acceptance speech.

For music, ask a friend who played guitar or piano for the production to start a jam session, or just turn up the stereo system and dance your butts off like crazy people who don't have to go to rehearsal tomorrow.

PHOTO STATION

At the entrance to your party, create one of those red-carpet event backdrops where the stars stop for photo ops. The backdrop can be made of a white sheet that has photocopies of the play's logo pasted onto it in a repeating pattern. See if you can scrounge up a velvet rope and a long carpet from the prop closet or a local thrift store for added effect. Plan to have the show's photographer take fun, posed arrival shots of each person walking in to the party, or do the honors yourself.

77 Scrapbooking Party

Back before the camera was invented, people preserved the special moments of their lives by filling albums with newspaper clippings, love letters, pressed flowers, quotes, poems, drawings, and souvenirs. Now that you've built up years of memories with your friends, you probably have heaps of that stuff, plus a ton of treasured snapshots. But how often do you look at any of it? Now's the perfect time to have your clan over for a scrapbooking "crop"—a party where each of you will create your own keepsake album of your shared history.

Prep

There are loads of decorative papers, tools, and embellishments (from metal rivets to rhinestone appliques to super techy die-cutting machines) that you can use, but it all gets expensive. Decide on a budget, then check the box to the right for a list of basics to provide for the party. Ask for donations from participants if you can't foot the bill alone. Also, pick up a few scrapbooking magazines full of sample layouts for your friends to flip through for inspiration at the party.

It's best to keep this as a small gathering of the pals with whom you share the most memories. Tell everyone to pick their six or so absolute favorite photos from your time together and bring replicated prints of those six for each person. They should also bring any memorabilia they've kept over the years—movie or concert ticket stubs, a takeout menu from your favorite diner, a miniature-golf scorecard—along with an empty album that has plain paper pages and/or large clear plastic sleeves (not sticky, self-adhesive pages or individual photo slots).

Do

Once you've all traded photos so that everyone has a complete identical set, spread out your supplies on a table and go to town! Attach your photos with adhesive photo corners or a photo-safe glue stick. Instead of gluing down precious mementos, preserve them by creating pockets for them to go in (glue three sides of a square of paper or cardstock to the page to make a pocket). If there's a funny story or deeper meaning behind a photo, handwrite the background info on a piece of paper with a nice pen and then glue it to the page as part of the layout.

Shopping List

Here are some suggestions for what to buy or borrow for your party.

• Scrapbook album (have each guest bring their own) • Several glue sticks marked acid-free, archival, or photo-safe • Several pairs of scissors • Self-adhesive photo corners (to affix photos without applying glue directly on them) • A selection of patterned papers for cutting out decorations, borders, and pockets • A couple sheets of alphabet stickers • Two or three different-colored fine-tip markers • One or two sheets of embellishments that fit your crew, like a set of soccer ball stickers or graduation-themed paper cutouts

78 Open Mic Night

Did you know that Lady Gaga got her start playing open mic nights as a teenager at clubs in New York? Everyone has to start somewhere, so provide your soon-to-be-discovered friends with their first gig: Spearhead your own open mic night where they can perform their best jokes, songs, poetry, or whatever for a real live crowd.

Prep

You can hold the event at a friend's house (with just people you know) or at a local coffee shop (where you'll get a wider audience). Both are good options. If you go the cafe route, pitch the idea to the manager by saying the event will drum up extra business on a slow weeknight.

Participants sign up for traditional open mics when they show up (they put their names on a list), but at a private party, you might want to sign up people in advance to make sure you have a full roster of acts. When you send out the invite, ask people to RSVP with what they're going to do (sing, play an instrument, do stand-up, read a poem they wrote, etc.) and how much time they will need (keep it under 15 minutes so everyone gets a chance). Then make a schedule. You could organize the evening around a theme—like "love gone wrong" or "aliens and animals"—which might help people come up with ideas for what to perform.

Make sure that the place where you're holding the event is equipped with a microphone and an amplifier. If it's not, rent or borrow them from a friend or your school.

Do

It'll be your job to MC the event, which means introducing each act and rallying applause if need be. If you're letting more performers sign up that night, put out a pen and the schedule, which should show the free slots. Test the sound equipment at the start of the night, and make sure things run smoothly throughout the event.

Get Competitive

A traditional open mic is just for fun, but if your friends are more serious about their art and up for some friendly competition, try these variations on the theme.

Poetry Slam. A spoken word competition where the audience is encouraged to react however they see fit during or after a poem—cheering if they like it, and if not, booing till the poet gives up! Crowd favorites are brought back up for subsequent rounds.

Battle of the Bands. Garage bands compete against one another with a winner selected either by the applause of the crowd, a panel of judges, or both (for example, the judges' votes make up 50 percent of the score and the audience's vote—via cheers—makes up the other 50 percent).

79 Fashion Statement Party

People don't always have the time, energy, or cash to pull together a great outfit for a costume party. But there's another way to go about it. Instead of requiring elaborate costumes, impose a clever fashion "rule" that forces guests to get creative with the stuff already in their closet (or kitchen, or garage).

Prep

To start, decide on a theme. Here are a few suggestions.

One Article Only. Guests may wear no more than a single item of clothing, like overalls, a full bodysuit, or a one-piece bathing suit.

Rubik's Cube. Each piece you wear—pants, shirt, hat, shoes—should be a different solid color. At the party, swap garments with other guests throughout the night till you're all one color from head to toe.

ABC. That stands for Anything But Clothes: Outfits can be made of any material—duct tape, newspaper, balloons, gum wrappers—except traditional items of clothing.

The Clash. Wear all your stripes, polka dots, madras, mismatched socks, and bright colors at once—the worse they look together, the better.

Doppelganger. Come with a friend dressed in an identical outfit; encourage guests to match more than just a shirt and pants.

Always a Bridesmaid. Come in your gown or tux from a past wedding party or prom, or pick up a super tacky one from the thrift store.

Tight and Bright. Neon and spandex rule at this party, where the goal is to wear the most snug, Technicolor outfit possible.

Traffic Light. Wear green if you're single, red if you're taken, and yellow if it's, uh, complicated.

Whatever your theme, have some extra costume pieces—like garbage bags for ABC or crazy ties for The Clash—for those who show up in regular garb.

Clothes Call Playlist

"Fashion" (Lady Gaga) • "Dress You Up" (Madonna) • "Fashion Victim" (Green Day) • "Freakum Dress" (Beyoncé) • "Fashion" (David Bowie) • "Fashion Is Danger" (Flight of the Conchords) • "Clothes Off!!" (Gym Class Heroes) • "Hot in Herre" (Nelly)

Do

Consider naming winners in various costume categories. At Rubik's Cube, as with the classic '80s game, the first to solve their own puzzle gets the crown. At ABC, give out ribbons for Most Eco-Friendly, Most Uncomfortable-Looking, and the Mrs. [insert-your-junior-high-home-ec-teacher's-name-here] Award for Sewing Machine Skills. And at Doppleganger, the most identical pair earns a prize.

80 Thailand: Full Moon Party

Once a month on the full moon, up to 30,000 people from around the world flood onto Haad Rin beach on the Thai island of Koh Phangan for the all-night beach rave known as the Full Moon Party. Re-create the fun at your own celebration the next time the moon is full.

Prep

Figure out the dates of the full moons over the summer, and pick one. If there's a beach nearby that allows nighttime parties, bonfires, and camping, hold your event there—otherwise, a backyard works just as well. Guests should stay over if possible, since the goal of the full moon party is to dance till sunrise. Realistically, everyone will need to take a break at various points. If your party's at a house, create a chill-out room with everyone's sleeping bags and pillows along with snacks and drinks.

On Haad Rin beach, you'd also see pros dancing and juggling with fire. You definitely don't want to imitate their daring feats with actual flames, but you can create a similar vibe with glow sticks and other neon toys, like hula hoops, poi (balls on strings that you twirl), and staffs (large batons that you spin).

Serve

Dancing all night makes you thirsty, so you'll need lots of soda, juice, and water. Serve it Koh Phangan-style—in buckets! Get a bag of large straws and go to the dollar store for the smallest plastic beach pails you can find. For food, have some Thai takeout delivered, like pad thai or curry followed by sticky rice with mango for dessert. Or just pick up some mangos—dried or fresh—and some chili-spiced nuts. Also, see the recipe below.

Do

As your friends arrive, descend on them with neon orange, green, and pink body paints. Apply them in tribal stripes as war paint (staying up till dawn *is* a battle). Then let the dancing begin! Make a bunch of playlists and/or ask several friends to take DJ shifts throughout the night so that the music never stops—at Full Moon, the vibe is typically dance, trance, techno, and reggae.

Thai Chili Lime Peanuts

Toss raw peanuts with a little bit of olive oil, sugar, and coarse salt, then roast on a baking sheet in a 350-degree oven for about half an hour, stirring every now and then. Next, dump them into a bowl and stir in two teaspoons of lime juice, a teaspoon of hot pepper sauce, and some cayenne pepper. Cool and store till showtime.

81 Scandinavia: Midsummer Party

Across Scandinavia (which comprises Sweden, Norway, Denmark, Iceland, and Finland), the summer solstice, also known as Midsummer, is a major holiday that falls on the third Friday in June. Winters are brutal and dark in Scandinavia, but because the region is so far north, the sun barely sets at all on Midsummer's Eve, creating all-night twilight conditions—the perfect mood lighting for a party. We may not have midnight sun in the US, but the longest day of the year is still cause for celebration.

Prep

Midsummer parties are generally held outside by a body of water, so try and have your party near a lake or ocean. If that's not possible, a backyard will work. The solstice is seen as a welcome of summertime and the season of fertility—so think romantic with the décor. In Sweden, a maypole is the centerpiece of the festivities; it's a big cross that's wrapped in flowers and plants, with two wreaths hanging from either arm, and everyone dances around it. You can use a flagpole, tetherball pole, badminton net pole, or deck post, too. Since you won't have the benefit of all-night sun, hang mason-jar candle lanterns from the trees to illuminate the space (use LED tealight "candles" to prevent fire).

Wear

Wildflowers and plants are a big part of Midsummer celebrations; girls wear pretty garlands around their heads, as do some guys (or they wear ones made of leaves). Gather or buy some blossoms and greenery ahead of time for your friends to tuck behind their ears or weave into daisy chains.

Summer Night Playlist

"Nightswimming" (R.E.M.) • "Fireflies" (Owl City) • "Summer Nights" (John Travolta & Olivia Newton-John) • "Summer Love" (Justin Timberlake) • "All Summer Long" (Kid Rock) • "The Boys of Summer" (The Ataris) • "In the Summertime" (Mungo Jerry) • "Summer Breeze" (Jason Mraz) • "Summertime" (DJ Jazzy Jeff & The Fresh Prince)

Serve

The traditional meal of Midsummer is pickled herring and sour cream, new potatoes with dill, and fresh strawberries and cream. Of course, you can amend the menu to just include potato chips and strawberry shortcake—your guests probably won't protest!

Do

Midsummer's Eve is thought to be a magical time for love. Single girls at the party can collect seven different flowers before the evening is through, then place them under their pillows, with hopes that they'll dream of their future spouse that night. Eating salty foods is also said to inspire your mystery lover to bring you water in your sleep. Bonfires are favorite traditions for solstice celebrations; so if you have access to a fire pit, light it up!

82 Brazil: Carnaval Drum & Dance Party

Carnaval—otherwise known as the "greatest party on earth"—is a four-day-long affair in Rio de Janeiro, Brazil. Like Mardi Gras (page 48), it celebrates the week before the solemn Christian holiday of Lent, but it's more focused on music and dance than on beads and debauchery. Here's how to replicate a little piece of the pageantry at your own Carnaval party.

Prep

In Carnaval, people form groups known as *blocos* (Portuguese for "blocks"), which march down the streets and boast percussion bands that usually play samba music. Create a similar atmosphere at your party by getting a drum circle going; tell people on the invites to bring drums along. Traditional samba drums include the surdu, cuica, timbal, and caixa, but any percussion instrument will work, including bongos, tambourines, and cymbals. In addition, put out empty plastic buckets, stock pots, and wooden spoons, and anything else that can be used to bang out a beat.

Do

To get started, sit in a circle with your drums. Ask one person to play a basic beat and let everyone else weave in their own rhythm one by one. (If your friends aren't a very musical crowd, just throw on the playlist to the right and drum to that.) Anyone not making music is free to dance away. Try dancing the traditional Samba. To see how it's done, look up videos online.

Wear

Have people coordinate with a few close friends to come as a *bloco*. Beforehand, they should come up with a funny name that suits their group (some examples from the actual Carnaval are Christ's Armpit, and Nana Banana), and then arrive at the party in matching outfits. While many Carnaval costumes resemble those of Vegas showgirls—complete with feathers, sequins, and headdresses—some block party participants simply wear T-shirts with matching logos. Tell your friends they can go as elaborate or as low-key as they want!

Samba Playlist

"Escola de Samba (Pedindo Passagem)" (Luciano Perrone) • "Coisinha do Pai" (Beth Carvalho) • "Beijo Na Boca" (Banda Beija) • "E Samba" (Junior Jack) • "Samba Novo" (Rosalia de Souza) • "The In Samba" (Nicola Conte) • "Batucada" (Escola Do Bahia) • "Carro Velho" (Banda Eva) • "Água Mineral" (Timbalada)

Eat

As your drummers and dancers work up an appetite, serve Brazilian finger foods like pão de queijo (small rolls baked with cheese), pastéis (deep-fried pastry pockets filled with cheese, meat, or fruit), and coxinhas (shredded chicken salad that's been molded into the shape of a drumstick, battered, and fried). If you don't have an ethnic grocery store nearby, look up recipes and try making them yourself.

83 Mexico: Cinco de Mayo Fiesta

Spanish for May 5, Cinco de Mayo commemorates the day back in 1862 when the underdog Mexican army defeated the French in a town called Puebla during the second Franco-Mexican War. The Mexicans didn't win that war, but they won the battle, and since then, the day has come to symbolize triumph against great odds. Today, the celebration of Cinco de Mayo is even greater in the US than it is in Mexico, as it's become a holiday during which the US shows support of its Mexican community and Latino culture.

Prep

Go with the colors of the Mexican flag—red, white, and green—wherever you can. Use an Aztec-patterned blanket as a tablecloth on your buffet, and decorate with paper picado. If you can't find them anywhere, make them yourself.

Serve

The biggest focus at a Mexican-themed party is the food. Fill your grocery cart with tortilla chips and serve them with an array of dips: guacamole, salsa, salsa con queso, black bean dip, and sour cream. For an easy main dish to serve buffet style, do make-your-own fajitas, burritos, or tacos. Just lay out the tortillas on one end of the table, followed by trays of individual toppings (ground beef, shredded cheese, refried beans, chopped lettuce and tomatoes, and any of the dips above). For drinks, make a picther of virgin margaritas. Run a lime wedge around the rims of all your glasses, then dip them onto a plate of coarse salt, and line them up ready for your guests to fill.

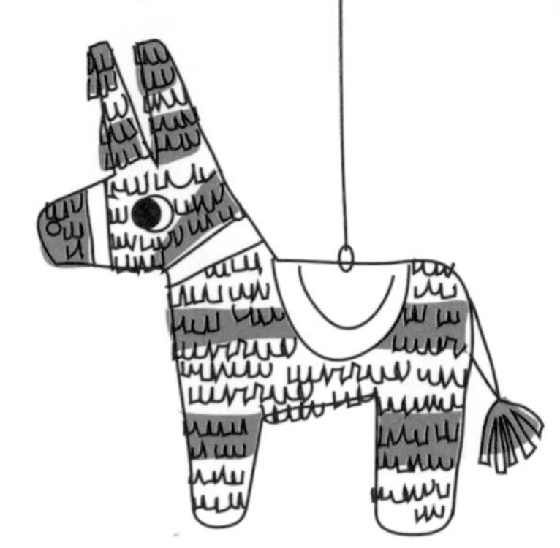

Do

What kind of fiesta would it be without a piñata? Find a traditional Mexican symbol (like a donkey), and fill it with things like sticks of lip balm, scratch-off lottery tickets, and anything else that's small and cheap and fun.

If eating, dancing, and beating the life out of a papier-mâché burro isn't enough, have a chile-eating contest: Pick up a bunch of different chile peppers at your grocery or ethnic food store and line them up in order of hotness. Get three daredevil volunteers to go head-to-head to see who can eat the most, the fastest—you may want to provide glasses of milk (much better than water for relieving the burn), a bucket for spitting, and tissues for the tears!

Viva Mexico Playlist

"La Bamba" (Ritchie Valens) • "Guantanamera" (Los Lobos) • "Low Rider" (War) • "Alocatel" (Mexican Institute of Sound) • "Más" (Kinky) • "Lucky (Suerte)" (Jason Mraz & Ximena Sariñana) • "Como Tú" (Jaguares) • "Tu Carcel" (Los Bukis) • "Bien o Mal" (Julieta Venegas) • "Oye Mi Amor" (Maná) • "Mientes" (Camila)

84 Ireland: St. Patrick's Day Party

Though it started as a religious Catholic holiday that honored St. Patrick (the patron saint of Ireland), St. Patrick's Day, also known as St. Patty's Day, has become a huge non-secular celebration in the US that revolves around being with friends, wearing green, and partying hard! It's held in early spring, every March 17 (the day St. Patrick died back in the year 460). Nobody minds too much when partiers take liberties with Celtic traditions and symbols—as long as it's in the name of good fun.

Prep

Decorate with green! This is the quintessential color of St. Patty's Day, as it represents the shamrocks the saint used to explain the holy trinity (father, son, and holy spirit) to his students. In addition, create a leprechaun's pot of gold, an iconic symbol from Irish folklore, by taking a cast-iron kettle or a Halloween-prop cauldron and filling it with gold-wrapped loot like chocolates. Draw, cut out, and mount a half-rainbow shape leading to the pot. Decorate the wall with shamrocks and expressions like "Irish Eyes are Smiling," "Luck of the Irish," and "Erin go Bragh" (which means "Ireland Forever").

Wear

Well, green. But don't leave it at that. Play off the "Kiss me, I'm Irish" thing by making a grab-bag of buttons for all your friends with variations like "Tickle me, I'm Irish" and "Fist-bump me, I'm Irish." Do them totally low-tech by printing out the words on your computer, cutting them out in a circle, and simply gluing them over other cheap buttons. Or use a fabric pen on green felt cut into circles or shamrock shapes, and stick safety pins through them.

Sham-Rock Playlist

"Sunday Bloody Sunday" (U2) • "Nothing Compares to You" (Sinead O'Connor) • "Dreams" (The Cranberries) • "Brown Eyed Girl" (Van Morrison) • "That Woman's Got Me Drinking" (Shane MacGowan & The Popes) • "Sally MacLennane" (The Pogues) • "The Wild Rover" (Dropkick Murphys) • "American Land" (Bruce Springsteen) • "Devil's Dance Floor" (Flogging Molly)

Do

In Ireland, tradition holds that anyone who kisses the Blarney Stone, a block in the wall of Blarney Castle in County Cork, receives the "gift of gab" (that is, they become a smooth talker—whether they use the skill to go into politics or sweet-talk a date). For your party, get someone to wear a T-shirt that says Blarney Stone or has a picture of Blarney Castle on it. Then make sure everyone gets a turn planting one on him or her.

Serve

You could stick to green, with single-color M&Ms and Jelly Bellies and such. But you could also go with a theme of potatoes (the food of Ireland!) and serve chips, skins, and fries of all shapes and sizes; don't forget a big platter of mashed potatoes. Corned beef and cabbage is a traditional Irish-American dish, if you want to make a full meal.

85 China: Chinese New Year Party

This holiday, which falls in January or February, is the most important one of the year in China. It's an occasion for fireworks, feasting, undulating dragon and lion dances, and in America, big, brightly colored parades.

Prep

Clean the space for your party well (in Chinese tradition, cleaning is thought to wash away whatever bad luck has piled up over the past year!) and decorate in red, China's signature lucky color. Hang a few round paper Chinese lanterns from the ceiling.

Serve

You can cook or get take-out—both are acceptable in China, but what's really important are the symbolic meanings behind the traditional dishes, meant to bring fortune and happiness in the New Year. Here are some suggestions for the menu: long noodles (which signify long life), sticky rice pudding cake (which is said to help you advance and prosper), and round dumplings (which bring the promise of wealth). Don't forget the fortune cookies! Consider coming up with your own funny fortunes and baking them inside homemade cookies, or ordering custom ones online. Wash it all down with cups of green tea.

Do

Like in America on the Fourth of July and India on Diwali (see Diwali Party, page 186), fireworks are a big part of many Chinese New Year celebrations. Traditionally, this custom was to scare off evil spirits and bring good fortune.

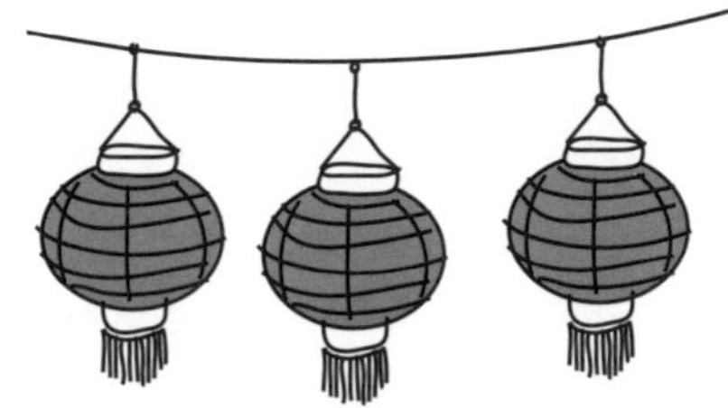

Since full-on fireworks aren't always legal or safe, hand out boxes of noise-making party snaps. The Chinese also give children red envelopes that hold cash on the New Year. Tweak the tradition by putting a different fortune or poem in each envelope, and placing them all in a basket for guests to pick from.

Party Animals

On the ancient Chinese calendar, each New Year is associated with one of 12 animals. Let the characteristics of the year's animal help provide inspiration for your party!

Year:	New Year's Day falls on:	Year of the:
2011	February 3	Rabbit
2012	January 23	Dragon
2013	February 10	Snake
2014	January 31	Horse
2015	February 19	Sheep
2016	February 9	Monkey
2017	January 28	Rooster
2018	February 16	Dog
2019	February 5	Boar
2020	January 25	Rat
2021	February 12	Ox
2022	February 1	Tiger

86 Spain: La Tomatina Party

It all started back in the 1940s when some Spanish kids got into a scuffle in the Buñol town square and hit up a nearby produce stand for "ammunition." Now, on the last Wednesday in August every year, thousands gather in the streets of Buñol for what's become arguably the world's best food fight, La Tomatina. Happy, half-naked tourists and locals alike are allowed—for exactly one hour—to hurl upwards of 300,000 pounds of tomatoes at one another, just for kicks. Use these tips to throw (no pun intended) your own killer food fight.

Prep

The place to have an event like this is in someone's backyard. Don't try to do it in a public park, and don't even think about having it indoors; the cleanup's not going to be pretty. Invite as many people as possible for maximum mayhem. Hit up a big wholesale or warehouse market for a mother lode of cheap tomatoes. Overripe ones will be the squishiest and kindest to your flesh when they hit you at top speed; ask to speak to the manager about a discount on the unsold produce they've just taken off the shelves. Before you put them out for the event, smush each one slightly to soften its blow.

Wear

To imitate the Spanish event, guys should come shirtless and girls should wear all white clothes they don't mind ruining. Everyone dons glasses, goggles, or snorkel masks since tomatoes irritate the eyes (though they're a natural smoothing treatment for the skin, which is a bonus).

Do

Throw tomatoes! Start with a ceremonial tomato juice-filled balloon volley between two teams. When one team drops the balloon, the other gets to throw the first tomato and start the free-for-all.

Serve

All those red, ripe tomatoes making you hungry? After the stash of ammunition has turned to pulp, serve up a heaping platter of spaghetti and marinara to refuel everyone. If you want to stay true to Spain, make it the rice dish *paella* instead.

More Messy Fests

Good, clean fun? Nah. Here's some additional inspiration for partying down and dirty.

Historical Carnival of Ivrea. In this northern Italy town, residents pelt each other with oranges during three days before Lent.

Oozfest. Each year, fire trucks hose down dirt courts at the State University of New York at Buffalo for what some claim is the country's largest mud volleyball game.

Holi. At this spring festival in India, people toss *gulal* (brightly colored powder) at one another until everyone looks like they were caught in an explosion at the Crayola factory.

87 India: Diwali Fest

Every year in either October or November, depending on the Hindu lunisolar calendar, people across India celebrate Diwali. It honors the triumph of good over evil, commemorating when (as told by legend) Prince Lord Rama killed the demon Ravana and returned to his people after 14 years in exile. The people lit the way for his return, and Diwali, an annual festival of lights, was born. Here's how to throw your own celebration of the five-day holiday—though you can start with just one night for now!

Prep

Diwali dates change yearly; check online to find out the right day to hold your party. The word "Diwali" translates to "row of lamps," so put out some *diyas* (little clay oil lamps), which symbolize the triumph of light over darkness. You can also simply buy some inexpensive tealights and display those instead. Use the candles and lamps sparingly since fire is always a concern, and decorate the rest of the space with electric twinkly lights.

Wear

Traditionally, you'd wear Indian dress to a Diwali party—*saris* for girls (a length of fabric draped around the waist and over one shoulder, worn on top of pants and a midriff-baring, short-sleeved top) and *kurtas* for guys (knee-length, long-sleeve tunics). It's not too hard to make your own sari or sari-like garment out of cloth from the fabric store. Girls can also draw *bindis*—small decorative dots that can signify marital status or represent the third eye in Hindu culture—on their foreheads.

Serve

Giving out sweets is the custom at Diwali. Stock up on pastries from a local or online Indian grocery. Or try making your own: Look up recipes for treats like *soan papdi* (sweet, flaky bars spiced with cardamom) and *gulab jamun* (fried milk balls in syrup).

Do

Diwali honors the Hindu goddess of wealth, Lakshmi, and welcomes prosperity in the coming year. So, gambling is a fun way to mark the occasion. Put out some decks of cards and poker chips, and let your friends go at it! *Mehndi*, the ancient Indian art of drawing intricate designs on the hands and feet, also makes a great party activity. These temporary tattoos are painted in a plant extract called henna that dries to a brownish-orange color and lasts for up to three weeks. Get some henna and stencils, and have your most artistic friend offer tattoos throughout the night.

Indian Party Playlist

"Jai Ho" (A.R. Rahman, Sukhvinder Singh, Tanvi Shah, Mahalaxmi Iyer & Vijay Prakash) • "Salaam Namaste" (Kunal Ganjawala, Vishal-Shekhar & Vasundhara Das) • "Kajra Re" (Alisha Chinoy, Javed Ali & Shankar Mahadevan) • "Dhoom Machale" (Sunidhi Chauhan) • "Hum to Bhai Jaise Hain" (Lata Mangeshkar)

About the Author

Melissa Daly is a freelance writer and former deputy editor of *Seventeen* magazine who has contributed to *Cosmopolitan*, *Fitness*, *Men's Health*, *Self*, *Shape*, *Prevention*, and *Redbook*. She is the coauthor of eight health and relationship books for tweens. She grew up partying in the woods and basements of Marlborough, Connecticut, before moving on to Greek life at the College of William & Mary, followed by 10 years in New York City's dive-y dance bars. She now lives in Portsmouth, New Hampshire.

About the Illustrator

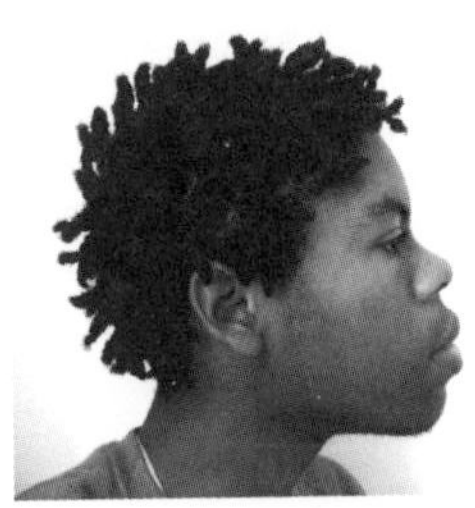

Christian Robinson loves to make things. Born and raised in Los Angeles, California, he received a BFA in character animation from the California Institute of the Arts and has interned with Pixar Animation Studios and the Sesame Street Workshop. He currently works as a freelance artist and lives in San Francisco, California.

Author Acknowledgments

Thanks to my editors Hadara Graubart and Karen Macklin for their patience (sorry, I had to party!).

A shout-out as well to all the friends who contributed ideas and whose invite lists I hope to always be on, especially Anthony, Ash, Dave, Monique, Margaret, the W&M Thetas, Pikas, and Pi Lams, and the RHAM, Hartford County 4-H, and Med-O-Lark contingents. Love to Joe, who's built the best hang-out house ever.

Special thanks to my mom and dad for listening and knowing that sometimes, you gotta fight for your right …

Other Zest Books

97 Things to Do Before You Finish High School

by Steven Jenkins and Erika Stalder

The Look Book

50 Iconic Beauties and How to Achieve Their Signature Styles

by Erika Stalder with celebrity hair and makeup artists Christopher Fulton and Cameron Cohen

Queer

The Ultimate LGBT Guide for Teens

by Marke Bieschke & Kathy Belge

Freshman

Tales of 9th Grade Obsessions, Revelations, and Other Nonsense

by Corinne Mucha

Start It Up

The Complete Teen Business Guide to Turning Your Passions Into Pay

by Kenrya Rankin

Fashion 101
A Crash Course in Clothing

by Erika Stalder

The Date Book
A Girl's Guide to Going Out With Someone New

by Erika Stalder

Indie Girl
From Starting a Band to Launching a Fashion Company, Nine Ways to Turn Your Creative Talent Into Reality

by Arne Johnson & Karen Macklin

Reel Culture
50 Classic Movies You Should Know About (So You Can Impress Your Friends)

by Mimi O'Connor

Take Me With You
Off-to-College Advice From One Chick to Another

by Nikki Roddy